Burgundy

A wine lover's touring guide

Already published:
Alsace

Forthcoming titles in this series:
Bordeaux
Loire
Rhône
Provence
Jura/Savoie
Champagne
Languedoc/Roussillon
The Southwest
Corsica

If no address is given for a hotel, park, wine cellar or other place of interest, the reader may assume that everyone in the locality will be able to give directions or that signs point the way.

Hubrecht Duijker

Burgundy

A wine lover's touring guide

Het Spectrum

Books by Het Spectrum are brought onto the market by:
Publishing House Het Spectrum Ltd.
Postbus 2073
3500 GB Utrecht
The Netherlands

Cover design: Alpha Design, Leusden, The Netherlands
Photos: Hubrecht Duijker, photo on page 47b: Andrë Ziltener
Translation: Paul Goodman
Lay out/Typesetting: Meijster Design, Haarlem, The Netherlands
Lithography: RCA, Zwolle, The Netherlands
Cartography: TOP 250 n° 108 en 109 © IGN Paris 1992 - Autorisation n° 30.3031
Printing: Aubin Imprimeur, Ligugé, France
First edition: 1993
Cover photo: Hotel-Dieu in Beaune.

The author will be grateful for any suggestions, ideas and comments concerning this guide. You may send them to the above address, attn. Hubrecht Duijker.
Many thanks to the Comité Régional du Tourisme in Dijon and the B.I.V.B. in Beaune.

ISBN 1 85365 306 3

British Library Cataloguing-in-Publication Data.
A catalogue record for this book is available from the British Library.

Contents

Chenôve
Pouilly-en-Auxois
Créancey
Commarin
Échannay
Châteauneuf
Arnay-le-Duc
Gevrey-Chambertin
Fixin
Chambolle-Musigny
Clos de Vougeot
Vosne-Romanée
Nuits-St-Georges
Savigny-lès-Beaune
Aloxe-Corton
Beaune
Hôtel-Dieu
Pommard
Meursault
Auxey-Duresses
Bligny-sur-Ouche
Nolay
la Rochepot
Santenay
Chagny
Puligny-M
Rully
Mercurey
Givry
Germolles
CHALON-S.-SAÔNE
St-Marcel
LE CREUSOT
Montchanin
Couches
Buxy
Mont-St-Vincent
Tournus
Cuisery
Sennecey-le-Grd
Verdun-s.-le-Doubs
Cussigny
Quincey
Bagnot
Combertault
Allerey-sur-Saône
Bey
Montcoy
St-Christophe-en-Bresse
la Frette
Mgne des Trois-Croix
Forêt de Gergy
Forêt de la Ferté
Sully
Saisy
Epinac
Jours-en-Vaux
Archéodrome
A 36-E 60
A 6-E 15-E 21
A 6-E 15-E 60
A 31
A 38
N 6
N 74
N 80-E 607
Saône
Dheune

Tournus
Cuisery
Cormatin
Chapaize
Brancion
Ozenay
Cluny
Anc. Abbaye
Mont St-Romain
Blanot
Bissy-la-M.
Cruzille
Uchizy
Farges-les-Mâcon
le Villars
Pont-de-Vaux
St-Albain
Berzé-le-Châtel
Berzé-la-Ville
Milly-Lamartine
Bussières
Pierreclos
St-Point
Tramayes
Matour
Charnay-lès-M.
Solutré-Pouilly
Roche de Solutré
MÂCON
Replonges
Bâgé-le-Châtel
St-André-de-Bâgé
Juliénas
Chénas
Romanèche-Thorins
Fleurie
Villié-Morgon
Avenas
Beaujeu
Chénelette
Belleville
St-Georges-de-Reneins
Salles-Arbuissonnas-en-Beaujolais
St-Julien
Chambost-Allières
VILLEFRANCHE-SUR-SAÔNE
Beauregard
Chamelet
Jarnioux
Oingt
Theizé
Ternand
Anse
Bagnols
Charnay
St-Jean-des-Vignes
Chât. d'Avauges
Bully
l'Arbresle
Sevigny
Poleymieux-au-Mt-d'Or
69
Brienon-sur-Armançon
St-Florentin
Germigny
Pontigny
Anc. Abb.
Seignelay
Ligny-le-Châtel
Maligny
Chablis
AUXERRE
Chitry
St-Bris-le-Vineux
Escolives-Ste-Camille
Irancy
Coulanges-la-Vineuse
Cravant
Vermenton
Ste-Pallaye
Prégilbert
Anc. Abb. de Régny
Sacy
Mailly-le-Château
Arcy-sur-Cure
Grottes d'Arcy
89

Introduction

Burgundy was once a large duchy to which parts of Belgium, Holland and Luxemburg belonged but nowadays it consists of five departments in eastern France: Ain, Côte d'Or, Nièvre, Saône-et-Loire and Yonne. The wine region of Burgundy occupies only a relatively modest area of 40,000 hectares (Bordeaux amounting to some 100,000 hectares). In addition, more than half of the Burgundian vineyards do not actually lie within Burgundy itself because they belong to Beaujolais in the department of Rhône. There are striking differences between geographic Burgundy and those areas related by wine. It is extra confusing that many wine lovers refer to only one of the five wine districts (the Côte d'Or) by the term 'Burgundy'. Those who wish to understand Burgundy and its almost one hundred different wines have a hard task ahead of them because this is one of the world's most complex wine districts. There is enormous fragmentation of landed property here and more will be said about this in the chapter concerning viniculture and wines.

A wine route through the Mâconnais.

Chablis and Cote d'Or

Traditionally, Burgundy is divided into five districts. In the north, isolated from the others, lies *Chablis* (bordered by a few vineyards). From Paris it can easily be reached via the A 6. The same *autoroute* connects the district of Chablis with that of the *Côte d'Or*. In both history and atmosphere, this is the heart of Burgundy. Here the best and most famous wines, red and white, are made. The Côte d'Or district consists mainly of vineyards that follow the eastern slopes of a low, broad mountain chain towards the south.

In the Côte d'Or lies Beaune, considered to be the wine capital of Burgundy. Many wine dealers have their premises here, and have done so for centuries. Official wine agencies are also established in Beaune (although none are from Beaujolais) and the largest charity auction in the world takes place here annually on the third Sunday of November, when the wines of the collective hospitals of Beaune (the Hospices de Beaune) are sold. Due to its location, in the middle of the Côte d'Or, at the intersection of two *autoroutes* from the north, Beaune serves as an overnight stop for large numbers of tourists. The city has thousands of hotel rooms at its disposal. The administrative capital of Burgundy, Dijon, is situated directly to the north of the wine district.

Chalonnais

Almost all the vineyards of the wine district of the Côte d'Or lie within the department of the same name, the only exception being those with the *appellation* Maranges, in the extreme south, which are situated in the Saône-et-Loire department. From the three districts that form Maranges, it is only a few kilometres to the northernmost fields of *Chalonnais*, the next district. This is also called Côte Chalonnaise. In shape it resembles a tall, rather narrow rectangle. The wines – red and white – are less rich than those from the Côte d'Or but also cost less. In the Chalonnais, Crémant de Bourgogne, a sparkling wine, is also made.

Maconnais

To the south, Chalonnais merges almost unnoticeably into *Mâconnais* which takes the form of a bunch of grapes: broad at the top and narrower below. The narrow, southern tip is full of hills and valleys and it is here that the most famous wine of the district is found: white Pouil-

Bacchus pours wine in Viré.

ly-Fuissé. White wine plays a major part throughout Mâconnais, and is noted for its quality and the amount produced.

Beaujolais

The southernmost vineyards of Saône-et-Loire belong to the largest of the five Burgundian districts, *Beaujolais.* Further on, they run for dozens of kilometres through the department of Rhône until just north of Lyon. To the west Beaujolais is flanked by a large mountain range, while the extinct volcano of Mont Brouilly stands in the middle of the department. Beaujolais is the most romantic of the Burgundian districts, especially the villages, where time seems to have stood still. The lively and fruity Beaujolais, once a fairly unimportant regional wine, has developed into one of the world's most famous wines. A substantial amount of the harvest is sold as Beaujolais Primeur or Beaujolais Nouveau after the third Thursday in November.

The church Saint-Vincent in Chalon-sur-Saône.

The Dangers of Night Frosts

It is about 300 kilometres from the northernmost to the southernmost point of the Burgundian vineyards. An extended area such as this shows great differences in landscape and climate. In and around Chablis there are limestone hills and the night frost is extremely dangerous for the grapevines. It is only thanks to modern treatments for combating frost that Chablis still exists and flourishes as a wine district. When frost threatens in springtime, heaters and fires are lit and sprinkler systems are set up in various locations. The water on the grapevines does indeed freeze but the vines themselves do not. Due to the danger of frost, almost all of the vineyards in Chablis and the surrounding district are set out on slopes and plateaus, because the cold is more extreme in low, flat areas.

Like Pearls on a Necklace

Detail from a mural in Buxy.

In the Côte d'Or the vineyards run from high up in the deforested hills to the valley around the N 74, which cuts straight through the district. All the important wine villages (and a few cities, such as Nuits-Saint-Georges and Beaune) are situated in a line from the north to the southwest. Gaston Roupnel once described them as 'pearls on a necklace'. The landscape of the Côte d'Or is not very exciting. Except during harvest time, most of the villages are very quiet and the uninitiated would hardly suspect that many of the world's best and most precious wines lie in the cellars here. Many doors and entrances are closed and nameplates are often missing. The reason for this is that the best winegrowers have a continual shortage of wine and thus do not need to let prospective customers taste their wares. The landscape of the Côte d'Or becomes increasingly lovely and varied the further into the hills you go. Above all, the countryside surrounding Hautes-Côtes – of which the wines have two separate *appellations* – is worth discovering. The climate of the Côte d'Or is quite mild.

Rustic Character

The monoculture of the winegrape is characteristic of the Côte d'Or. Things are different in Chalonnais, where vineyards border on fields of grain and vegetables as well as on pasture and forests. Hilly and level terrain alternates here. On the whole the landscape has a rustic atmosphere; the huge tourist wave of the Côte d'Or has not yet touched this region. The same holds for true Mâconnais, where the landscape at first looks very much like that of Chalonnais but is later accentuated by large hills and low mountains. The climate of Mâconnais has a slight Mediterranean feel. The roofs of the houses become flatter and more and more large balconies and terraces appear. In the area from which Pouilly-Fuissé originates, two steep rocks dominate the wine landscape. Numerous prehistoric finds have been made near Solutré.

A Green Landscape

Finally, there is Beaujolais, which consists of a long chain of hills, with a few level areas on the eastern side where the valley of the Saône is located. The beauty of the district much surpasses that of the other districts. Over and over again the winding, narrow roads offer varying views of wine slopes, wine valleys and wine villages. Some villages are built at the foot of hills, while others stand on hill tops. All of them wear the green habit of the grapevine because hardly any other plant species grow here. It is difficult to believe that Beaujolais once produced mainly grain. The only tangible reminder of this is the now vaneless windmill found in Moulin-à-Vent.

Romanesque Churches

Although remnants of prehistory, the Roman period and the Carolingian period can be found here and there, it is Romanesque architecture and sculpture that dominates in Burgundy. After the year 1000 – which was initially regarded as an ill-fated year – numerous churches were built or renovated under the influence of monastic orders. For about two centuries building was in the Romanesque style with its thick walls, small windows and vaulted, rather sober interiors. Another characteristic of this style is square, sturdy towers with narrow, arched windows and rather flat roofs. It is not surprising that many churches of this type were constructed in Burgundy because Cluny (Mâconnais) was the seat of the powerful Benedictine order. From here over 1000 to 2000 other monasteries were ruled throughout Europe. Romanesque art was introduced at the same time as Romanesque architecture and the capitals of churches were decorated with biblical and other images, which were primitive but at the same time expressive. There are so many Romanesque churches in Burgundy that a special route has been established for those who wish to visit them.

Flemish Influence

It was the Cistercian order (which had seceded from the Benedictines in 1115) that gave the impetus to Gothic architecture. This is lighter and finer than Romanesque architecture and its characteristics include cross vaults, pointed arches and flying buttresses. The Gothic architectural period in Burgundy lasted from about the middle of the 12th century until the end of the 13th century. Examples of Gothic churches will mainly be found in larger cities, such as Dijon. In the 14th century, people from Flanders and Holland came to Burgundy, among other reasons, to work in the ducal court. Many Flemish-Burgundian works of art, among which sculpture, paintings and multicoloured mosaic roofs, of which that of the Hôtel-Dieu in Beaune is the best-known example, date from this and the following century. In the course of the succeeding centuries, many castles, in all manner of architectural styles, including Classical, were built in Burgundy. Most of the castles within the wine area are found in Mâconnais and Beaujolais. It should be obvious to the visitor that the many delights from the wines can also be combined with a wide range of visual pleasures.

Historic Perspective

Few French winegrowing regions have a history as rich as that of Burgundy – a history that is reflected in numerous monuments, art treasures and buildings. In 52 BC the Gauls, led by Vercingetorix, were defeated at Alésia and Burgundy came under Roman rule. (The location of this historic siege is situated not far to the northeast of Semur-en-Auxois, a city near the A 6, between Auxerre and Beaune.) The Romans built new settlements and also expanded those already in existence. Cities such as Chalon-sur-Saône, Dijon and Mâcon were to rise from these settlements. Furthermore, the Romans introduced the art of winegrowing.
The collapse of the Roman Empire allowed an East Germanic tribe, the Burgundii, Burgunden or Burgonden, to settle in the area sometime around the beginning of the 5th century. This tribe founded a kingdom and thus gave Burgundy its name. A few decades later, the Franks conquered the area and the Merovingian period began. At that time, Burgundy was part of the Frankish kingdom, which was ruled by, among others, Charlemagne (768-814). The white wine Corton-Charlemagne (see the chapter on Aloxe-Corton) is named after him. The Frankish empire broke up in 843 and Burgundy ceased to exist as an independent entity. This continued until about two centuries later when, in 1031, Robert I the Elder was named duke of Burgundy. The Benedictine monastery of Cluny had been founded in 910 and a very powerful monastic order, which had an enormous influence on all aspects of life, developed from it. A second important monastic order, that of the Cistercians, arose in the 11th century with Cîteaux, situated not far from Nuits-Saint-Georges, as its centre. With the support of the monks, the dukes of Burgundy built their realm into a powerful state of great commercial and cultural importance.

A Powerful Duchy

The first Burgundian dukes were of the house of Capet. After this dynasty died out, the house of Valois came to power in 1364. Philip the Bold (Philippe le Hardi, so named because of his courageous behaviour during the Battle of Poitiers), then 14 years old, became duke. In 1369, he married Margaretha of Flanders, resulting in a duchy more than twice its original size. It stretched from Mâcon in the south

← *The vineyards round Odenas.*

to Friesland in the north and explains why many Flemish works of art are found in Burgundy. Philip even temporarily chose Brussels as his seat instead of Dijon. The exuberant lifestyle of the duke gave meaning to the term 'Burgundian'. He enjoyed eating and drinking enormously, introduced menus (at the time called *escriteau*) and banned the grape variety gamay which was of disappointing quality. It is even said that the word banquet originates from him, because at his court the nobles ate at horseshoe shaped tables surrounded by benches (*banque* is the French word for bench). Philip the Bold was succeeded by John the Fearless, Philip the Good and Charles the Bold (Charles le Téméraire). In 1475, the latter conquered the duchy of Lotharingen and the Dutch Gelre, so that, for the first time, Burgundy formed an almost united state between the French and German empires: the peak of Burgundian power had been reached.

Permanently French

Charles the Bold did not have much time left to enjoy this state of affairs, because he died two years later in Nancy. The French King Louis XI took advantage of the situation and seized a large part of Burgundy. At the same time he confiscated the entire harvest of the wine village of Volnay and transported it to his castle in Plessis-les-Tours. Not long afterwards, Maria, Charles the Bold's daughter, who resided in Ghent, married Maximilian of Habsburg. Outlying provinces such as Flanders, the Netherlands and Franche-Comté now became the property of the house of Habsburg – and the duchy of Burgundy was gone forever. The Habsburgs attempted to take Dijon over at the beginning of the 16th century but failed: the region was French and would remain so. Burgundy did, however, enjoy certain privileges, such as having its own governors (the princes of Condé) and its own parliament, situated in Dijon.

View of Chablis. →

Viticulture and Wines

The key to Burgundian winegrowing is that it is run on a small scale. After the French Revolution, the land was divided among the population by the religious and secular rulers and then further fragmented by inheritance rights. Because of this, Burgundy has almost no estates that are larger than 25 hectares. Fragmentation is greatest in the Côte d'Or.

The Role of the Wine Merchants

For many farmers the plots of land are too small to make or bottle wine themselves. This explains why the wine merchants, the *négociants-éleveurs*, play such an important role in the Côte d'Or. They collect the grapes, must or wine from dozens of small winegrowers, for the purpose of creating commercially viable quantities of the *appellations* concerned. It is estimated that two-thirds to three-quarters of the harvest in the Côte d'Or are put onto the market by wine merchants. The wine merchants of the Côte d'Or also produce wines from the other four districts, although a substantial amount of Beaujolais is brought onto the market by firms from that region.

In the Côte d'Or, co-operatives do not have an important role, unlike the situation in Chablis, Chalonnais, Mâconnais and Beaujolais. In

Late autumn near Chassagne-Montrachet.

The little village of Bailly, near Chablis.

Mâconnais 90 per cent of all wines are produced by *caves co-opératives*. Part of this volume is bottled by the firms themselves, but an even greater quantity goes to *négociants*.

Selection

Burgundy accounts for about 100 different *appellations*, of which most are in the Côte d'Or. Choosing the right wines from the large amounts offered is no picnic. Price plays a minor role: bad or average Burgundian wines usually cost just as much as good ones. Even the *appellation* does not give a guarantee of quality, because experience has taught that the same vineyard (with several owners) can produce widely varying wines. The production methods of wine merchants also vary greatly – therefor the quality of the wines does too. The reputation of the producer is much more important than either the price or the *appellation*: the quality of Burgundian wine is determined to a large extent by the human factor. This is why it is essential for restaurants, etc. to state not only the name of the Burgundian wine, but also its producer, on their wine lists. A few hundred only are mentioned in this guide.

Grape Varieties

Only a few grape varieties are cultivated in Burgundy. What's more, they are seldom mixed. There are four main varieties:
Chardonnay This is one of the world's most noble white grapes, originating from Burgundy itself. All the best Burgundian white wines are made from it (Chablis, the white wines of Côte d'Or and Chalonnais, Mâcon-Villages and other white Mâconnais, even white Beaujolais). Characteristic of a chardonnay wine is the aroma of tropical fruit but in Burgundy the wines often give a different impression, due to the influence of the soil and the use of oak casks.
Pinot Noir In Burgundy the chardonnay is to white wines what the pinot noir is to red wines: all great red wines are made from it. The grape produces rather elegant, soft, accessible Burgundian wines that are charming even when young. These wines frequently have an aroma that can be described as a delicious combination of floral and fruity tones. The aroma is also influenced by such things as the soil and the

Wine barrels being cleaned in Meursault.

possible lagering of the wine in oak casks.

Gamay While the pinot noir is characteristic of red Burgundian wines, the gamay is used to make Beaujolais. All red or rosé Beaujolais are made exclusively from this variety. Typical of a good gamay wine is a lively, fresh taste with an aroma of red berries and fruits; in particular this can be dramatically present in Beaujolais. In other districts of Burgundy the gamay noir à jus blanc – as it is called in full – is also produced, above all in Mâconnais. Apart from wines made solely from the gamay, a blended wine, Bourgogne Passetoutgrains, is also produced. This is made throughout the whole of Burgundy and is composed of two-thirds gamay and a third pinot noir.

Aligoté The fourth most planted grape is the white aligoté, which is made into Bourgogne Aligoté. This was formerly a rather sour, meagre wine but nowadays it usually tastes succulent, fruity and charming. Some of the best types come from the area surrounding Chablis (such as Saint-Bris-le-Vineux) and Hautes-Côtes.

Other Varieties Other grape varieties appear in Burgundy but in limited quantities. These include the white pinot blanc (it can give surprisingly good wines) and the kindred pinot gris, the sauvignon blanc (-gives the fresh, aromatic Sauvignon de St. Bris), as well as the simple white varieties sacy and melon de Bourgogne. There are also simple blue varieties called césar and tressot.

Wine Categories

On the basis of the grape varieties just mentioned, an extensive range of wines is produced; the French legislator recognizes about 100 different *appellations*. They can be roughly divided into five categories:

Regional Wines These are made throughout the whole of Burgundy: red and white Burgundy, Bourgogne Aligoté, Bourgogne Passetoutgrains and the sparkling Crémant de Bourgogne.

District Wines These can only be made in the (sub)districts concerned. Examples are Chablis, Côte de Beaune-Villages, Mâcon and Beaujolais.

The aligoté.

Municipal Wines These are wines from a single district or town or a group of districts: for example Gevrey-Chambertin, Beaune (Côte d'Or), Mercurey (Chalonnais), Pouilly-Fuissé (Mâconnais) and Fleurie (Beaujolais).

Near Saint-Aubin lies the hamlet of Gamay.

Premiers Crus Wines originating from a vineyard which is so classed. These are found in Chablis, Côte d'Or and Chalonnais.

Grands Crus The highest category. The Côte d'Or has about 30 vineyards with this title: Chablis has 7. The Côte d'Or wines of this sort are sold exclusively with the name of the vineyard alone, because it has its own *appellation* (Chambertin Clos de Bèze, Corton-Charlemagne). Chablis wines with this honorary title simply state Chablis Grand Cru along with the name of the vineyard.

A good restaurant.

The Cuisine

The people of Burgundy love the good life and sit down to dine with the greatest of pleasure, whether at home or in a restaurant. Hundreds of restaurants flourish in this region. Some of them are very luxurious and exclusive but the majority are simple and intended for the use of the inhabitants of the village. For this reason, a three-or four-course menu can be surprisingly inexpensive. Outside the tourist villages, prices are usually only about FF 100 – if not less.

Excellent Ingredients

Burgundian cuisine is, in essence, a domestic cuisine, based on old recipes handed down from mother to daughter. It is also a cuisine that makes full use of the many fresh ingredients that the region produces. These include beef from the famous, white Charolais cattle, raw hams from Morvan, crayfish, many types of saltwater fish, snails, mustard and a large range of cheeses: many of them goat cheeses (above all in Mâconnais and Beaujolais, although there is a most delicious variety called Montrachet) and the delectable Epoisses caraway cheese, sprinkled with Marc de Bourgogne. What's more, white Burgundy often tastes just as good when drunk with the regional cheeses as red Burgundy. The area also cultivates large quantities of vegetables and fruit, including blackberries, raspberries and cherries. From the first two fruits delicious liqueurs are made, called Crème de Cassis and Crème de Framboise.

A cheese-tasting locality in Nuits-Saint-Georges.

Specialities

On the basis of the ingredients just mentioned, the Burgundian chefs prepare specialities that taste just as marvellous as the accompanying wines. These include the nutritious *salade beaujolaise* with chicken

Andouillettes, a specialty of Chablis.

liver and bacon, *oeufs en meurette* (eggs poached in red wine), frogs' legs, *jambon persillé* (large pieces of ham in a white wine jelly with herbs such as parsley and garlic), *escargots de Bourgogne* (snails) and *andouillettes*, sausages for which numerous regional recipes exist. There are many different variations of *coq au vin*, if only because of the different types of wine. In every village in Beaujolais this dish is prepared using the local wine. *Poulet de Bresse* (also often called *volaille*) sometimes appears *à la crème* on the menu, with or without *morilles. Boeuf à la bourguigonne* or *boeuf bourguignon,* which is served in countless restaurants, is beef prepared in red wine, with onion, pieces of bacon and mushrooms. *Jambon à la lie de vin* is ham braised in the wine sediment that arises during fermentation. *Lapin rôti* (roast rabbit) is also encountered; mustard is often used in this dish. *Rable de lièvre* (saddle of hare) and many types of game, including *sanglier* and *marcassin* (wild boar and young wild boar, respectively). The excellent beef from Charolais is frequently offered in a variety of dishes, for example with wine sauce and marrow. Blackberries, and the liqueur made from them, are ingredients used in sweet desserts such as sherbets and pies. Those who enjoy Burgundian cuisine and wines understand why the French writer Curnonsky described this area as 'a gastronomic paradise'.

Poultry shop in Mâcon.

Using this Guide

This guide will take you through the whole of Burgundy, from Chablis in the north to deep in southerly Beaujolais. Information is given on every important wine village. The most important places of interest and other tourist facilities in each district are covered. Where useful and possible, hotels and restaurants are recommended, always with an indication of price. In general, the hotel prices are those for a double room. Titles of origin, wine producers or wine merchants are recommended for each village, sometimes with one or more of the best wines. This selection is one of the most complete ever made for Burgundy. All villages can best be explored on foot, however briefly. In this area the word 'hurry' should be scrapped from your vocabulary.

Hotels

When reserving a hotel room, always ask for a peacefully situated room, at the rear or overlooking a courtyard if possible. Watch out for loud and frequently rung church bells. At the time of reservation, you will be informed of your arrival time limit. If you intend to arrive later, telephone ahead, otherwise there is a chance that your room will be given to someone else. Written confirmation of a reservation is wise. Do this by letter or fax (ask for the number). In many villages in Burgundy (such as in Hautes-Côtes de Nuits) rooms may be rented privately. These residences can be recognized by signs (usually with *gîte*) and there is often a list of such addresses at the town hall or at the *syndicat d'initiative.*

Restaurants

It is absolutely essential that you telephone restaurants in advance, on the one hand to be sure of a table, and on the other hand to verify that it is open on that particular day. Experience has shown that it is sensible mainly to order from the *à la carte* menu, if only because it is cheaper. In addition, these are often made with market-fresh ingredients. In simple eating-houses, generally choose regional dishes, because the chef will probably struggle with complex or expensive recipes from elsewhere. Always choose regional wines and, if possible, wines from the village itself, because these will have been more expertly and critically chosen than wines from other areas. A carafe of water is always free, but mineral waters can also be ordered.

Winegrowers

It may take a good deal of effort to arrange to visit well-known winegrowers but the less well known will generally welcome you with pleasure. Do not hesitate to show them this guide: someone who comes through recommendation and also appears to be truly interested in wines is usually greeted in a friendlier way than a passing stranger. When tasting the wines – and in the Côte d'Or there are many – it is normal to spit them out but ask first where you can do this. Never give the winegrower a tip, but buy at least one bottle as a token of your appreciation for the hospitality enjoyed (naturally, this does not hold if you have paid for the visit, something that does happen now and then). In general French is the means of communication, although many young winegrowers speak English nowadays.

YONNE

The northernmost vineyards of Burgundy are situated in the department of Yonne, completely isolated from the others. Most of them are found around the city of Chablis, about 180 kilometres to the south-east of Paris. It is is more or less coincidence that Chablis belongs to Burgundy, because, in regard to location, climate and soil, it could just as well belong to Champagne. The best vineyards of the district of Chablis, like those of Champagne, contain a lot of lime. In Chablis, this thick lime layer is formed by the fossils of billions of shellfish, usually small oysters with a comma-shaped shell. The soil is called Kimméridgian, after Kimmeridge on the coast of Dorset, washed by the English Channel, because a similar layer is found there. It is the lime that gives the wines of Chablis – exclusively white – their special character. Wines made from chardonnay are characterized by their pale colour, often with a touch of green, and a very dry, somewhat mineral-like, cool taste which can be succulent and fruity at the same time. Furthermore, great Chablis wines ripen excellently. The best wines come from seven slopes directly to the north of Chablis: the grands crus Blanchots, Bougros, Les Clos, Grenouilles, Les Preuses, Valmur and Vaudésir. Somewhat less full, powerful and noble are the wines from the premiers crus, of which the wines from about 40 acres are sold under the name of individual or grouped vineyards. By far the largest amount of wine is that of Chablis without an epithet; about twice as much is made from this as from the grands crus and premiers crus put together. Finally, there is Petit Chablis, a wine that is modest both in quantity and quality and in which the characteristics of a true Chablis are hard to find.

The most interesting areas of the district of Chablis are described in the next few pages. There is also a separate chapter devoted to other wine villages in Yonne, where still as well as sparkling wines are produced.

Chablis

It is 12 kilometres from the *autoroute* (exit Auxerre-Sud) to Chablis. The winding road runs by way of *Beine* with its 12th- and 16th-century church. On the north side, a large lake has been excavated as a protection against night frost. Once in *Chablis,* the village square is easily found. To the north of the square is the Romanesque-Gothic church of Saint-Martin. The southern entrance is full of horseshoes, ex-votos from pilgrims asking the saint to heal their mounts. The Serein flows on the northeast side of Chablis. Walking in this direction you will come to an old street, the rue des Moulins, and l'Obédiencerie, a 15th-century building that once belonged to monks. There is a 13th-century wooden winepress here. The building is owned by the Domaine Laroche (visits by appoint-

The Romanesque-Gothic church of Saint-Martin.

Hotels

Hôtel de l'Etoile
✆ 86.42.10.50
Simple, pleasant rooms (14) with varying sanitary facilities, starting at about FF 300. Creaky hall floors. You can eat well in the restaurant.

Inexpensive menus commence at about FF 120. The emphasis is on regional dishes *(escargots, coq au vin d'Irancy,* regional *cheeses*). Wide choice of local wines, also older wines. Near the central square.

Hostellerie des Clos
✆ 86.42.10.63
The best hotel and restaurant of the district. About 25 tasteful rooms starting at FF 250. The light, large restaurant is excellent. The least expensive menu (around FF 165) offers particularly good value for your money. Wide wine selection. The owner, Michel Vignaud, is also the chef.

Les Lys
✆ 86.42.49.20

Recommended Producers

Billaud-Simon (Chablis). An important estate which owns many vineyards.
La Chablisienne (Chablis). Co-operative with about 250 members. Trustworthy wines.
G.A.E.C. de Chantemerle (La Chapelle-Vaupelteigne). Delicious, vital wines: Chablis, Chablis Fourchaume and Chablis l'Homme Mort.
René et Vincent Dauvissat (Chablis). Priceless, great wines. They age in oak casks. The range includes two grands crus and three premiers crus.
Jean-Paul Droin (Chablis). Over ten types of Chablis, almost all of good to

The grand cru vineyards, seen from Les Clos.

Functional, two-star hotel in south Chablis. Around 40 modern rooms starting at about FF 265.

Le Relais Saint-Vincent
Ligny-le-Chatel
✆ 86.47.53.38
Peaceful, small hotel with nice rooms (10) starting at about FF 200. Large breakfast. There is also a restaurant.

Restaurants

Auberge du Bief
Ligny-le-Chatel
✆ 86.47.43.42
Situated on a corner near the church by the the water. Rural as well as refined dishes. Menus start at FF 155.

ment). Chablis doesn't have many other old streets, because, in 1940, it was badly hit by bombs. The towers of the Porte Noël are reminders of a time when Chablis was walled and, thanks to wine, experienced great prosperity. In the southern part of the city is the historic 12th-century church of Saint-Pierre. By crossing the Serein and turning left, you come to the road leading to Maligny, with the slopes of the grands crus

Horseshoes on the church door.

very good quality.
Domaine de l'Eglantière (Maligny). The largest private wine estate in Chablis. The wines – in particular Chablis and premiers crus – are of an exemplary quality.
Domaine Laroche (Chablis). Modern complex in the south of the city. Large estate (owns the building l'Obédiencerie). High quality. The wines bought elsewhere are called Laroche.
Domaine de la Maladière (Chablis) Wide range of distinguished, priceless wines. The best ferment and age in oak casks.
Domaine des Malantes (Chablis) Beautiful, characteristic , high quality wines.

A stylishly decorated table.

to the right. Turn immediately right for *Fontenay-près-Chablis* (11th-century church, look at the rear). Then drive to Maligny. On the way you pass, on the left, the water pumping station for the sprinkler system that protects the grapevines against freezing. The castle of *Maligny*, situated in a

Le Syracuse
✆ 86.42.19.45
Inexpensive and tasty regional dishes (also *ouillette grillée*) from the butcher next door, e.g. *coq au St. Bris*. Large wine list. Situated on the village square.

Le Vieux Moulin
✆ 86.42.47.30
An inn located in an old watermill (rue des Moulins, across from the l'Obédiencerie). Regional cuisine, also *grillades*. Good wine list, reasonable prices (menus start at FF 100). Allied to the *Les Lys* hotel.

Au Vrai Chablis
✆ 86.42.11.43
A bar and restaurant on the village square. Delicious food for FF 100 and less. They also have tasty salads.

Winegrowers are easily found in La Chapelle Vaupelteigne.

Louis Michel & Fils (Chablis) Old family estate, complex wines (which can often age for a long time).
J. Moreau & Fils (Chablis) Large wine merchants with private land. The best wines come from here.
Domaine Pinson (Chablis) They work with traditional methods here. Thus the wines age in wooden casks.
François en Jean-Marie Ravenau (Chablis) Distinguished wines with a steely coolness and fine gradations. **A. Regnard & Fils** (Chablis) Property of Patrick de Ladoucette. This wine merchant produces fine, rather costly wines.
Simonnet-Febvre (Chablis) Small, seri-

large park, has been lovingly restored by the winegrower Jean Durup. In the centre, by an old market hall, is the 12th-and 14th-century church of Notre-Dame. *Ligny-le-Chatel*, the next wine village, has a striking church with a Romanesque nave, a chancel in Renaissance style and many religious works of art . By crossing the Serein once more and keeping to the right, you come to the road to *Pontigny.* A famous abbey can be found here, where the church was the largest Cistercian church of its time in France and one of the first Gothic buildings in Burgundy. Thanks to the monks of Pontigny, winegrowing flourished around Chablis. Drive back to Chablis by way of a tree-lined road to *Lignorelles* and from there take the fine route to *Villy.* Stop briefly in *La Chapelle-Vaupelteigne* in order to look at the old chapel and to enjoy the view. Near this wine village the remains of a Gallic-Roman settlement were found. To the south of Chablis, the churches of *Courgis* and *Préhy* are worth seeing. In Courgis, high up on a hill the ruins of a castle can also be found. From Préhy, there is a fine view across the wine landscape; the church is located in the midst of grapevines.

In Chablis you can taste to your heart's content.

TOURIST TIPS

- Chablis has a fine Office du Tourisme, which also supplies information about walking trips.

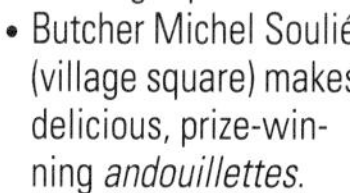

- Butcher Michel Soulié (village square) makes delicious, prize-winning *andouillettes.*
- In the street leading from the village square to the Porte Noël l'Art et le Vin is a gallery devoted to wine art.

ous business firm.
Domaine Vocoret (Chablis) Near the southern edge of Chablis.Excellent wines.
Also Recommended Dom. Collet (Chablis), G.A.E.C. du Colombier (Fontenay), Dom. des Courtis (Milly), Dom. Jean Defaix (Milly), Alain Geoffrey (Beines), Roland Lavantureux (Lignorelles), Dom. des Maronniers (Préhy), André Philippon (Fleys), Guy Robin (Chablis), Dom. Sainte Claire (Préhy), Gérard Tremblay (Poinchy), Dom. de Vauroux (Chablis).

RELATED TO WINE
Chablis's annual wine festival takes place On the fourth Sunday of November.

Restaurants

Le Saint-Bris
Saint-Bris-le-Vineux
✆ 86.53.84.56
You can eat very well here, in one of two nicely decorated dining rooms, for surprisingly little money. Even the Sunday à la carte menu costs less than FF 85. This cosy eating-house is situated near the church.

Les Vendanges
Coulanges-la-Vineuse
✆ 86.42.21.91
Simple village café and restaurant. For less than FF 100 you can satisfy even the biggest appetite. It also has a few rooms to rent.

Irancy nestles in a bowl-shaped wine valley.

Around Chablis

Just outside the district of Chablis there are a few areas where other wines are made. Crémant de Bourgogne (sparkling), Bourgogne Aligoté and white and red Bourgogne are produced here. The most important wine area is Saint-Bris-le-Vineux. It can be reached from Chablis by way of Courgis and *Chitry-le-Fort,* which has a fortified church. *Saint-Bris-le-Vineux* stands on the slope of a low hill. Many winegrowers' signs can be seen and many of the winegrowers have cellars dating from the 10th, 11th or 12th centuries. The local church has the allure of a cathedral. The wine speciality of Saint-Bris is Sauvignon de St. Bris, a cheerful, aromatic wine made from the white grape called sau-

The church of Saint-Bris-le-Vieux.

Recommended Producers

Saint-Bris-le-Vineux

Caves de Bailly (Bailly) Crémants de Bourgogne of top quality: white and rosé.
Domaine Bersan & Fils Pure, usually aromatic wines.
Robert en Philippe Defrance Fresh, tasty white wines.
Domaine Fort
Ghislaine et Jean-Hugues Goisot
Domaine des Remparts
Luc Sorin

Irancy

Léon Bienvenue
Bernard Cantin
René Charriat

Wine signs on the church square of Chitry-le-Fort.

vignon. By taking the D 956 in a southerly direction and then the exit for *Irancy*, you will soon arrive in this attractive wine village. The local wine bears the village name and is a light red. A small amount of wine is made from the blue grape, césar, which possibly originated here. By crossing the Yonne at Vencelottes, you drive straight to *Coulanges-la-Vineuse*. This village also produces light red wines, made solely from pinot noir. It is situated on a hill, around an 18th-century church with a tall, pointed tower dating from the 14th century. The village has a small Musée de la Vigne (ask about admittance at the town hall or in the *Les Vendanges* bar-restaurant).

Tourist Tips

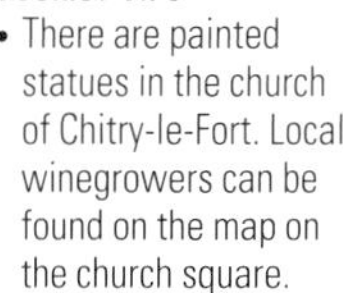

- There are painted statues in the church of Chitry-le-Fort. Local winegrowers can be found on the map on the church square.
- In Irancy there are the remnants of a few sections of the old town ramparts.

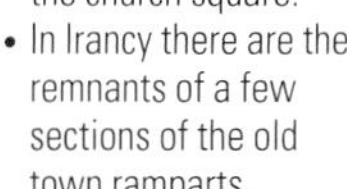

- You can drive into the Caves de Bailly. At the foot of the cellar complex runs the Yonne, with a narrow wharf and a bench.

Robert Colinot & Fils
Roger Delaloge
Jean Podor .
Coulanges-la-Vineuse
Raymond Dupuis
André Martin & Fils If the sun co-operates, the red wine can age for quite a few years.

Related to Wine

- On the weekend before November 11 Saint-Bris-le-Vineux usually celebrates the Fête du Sauvignon.
- In Auxerre, Epineuil, Joigny, Tonnerre, Vaux and Vézelay, both white and red Burgundies are produced in ever-increasing amounts.

Cote d'Or

The district of Côte d'Or is not only the heart of Burgundy but, for many, it is synonymous with Burgundy because, when wine lovers speak of 'Burgundy', they often mean Côte d'Or, in the same way as those who use the expression 'a Burgundy' have in mind a wine from this district. The most famous red and white Burgundies are made here. Furthermore, the dukes of Burgundy had their seat in the Côte d'Or, so the history of Burgundy is closely bound up with the district.
The wine district of Côte d'Or begins just below Dijon and ends about 50 kilometres past Santenay in a southwesterly direction. Almost the entire wine area lies within the department of the same name; only a few areas in the extreme south belonging to the department of Saône-et-Loire. The *appellation* of this group of villages is Maranges. The *route nationale* 74, which connects Dijon with Chagny, runs straight through the Côte d'Or. It is a busy road, which sometimes cannot be avoided but often can. For example, in the north, between Marsannay and Nuits-Saint-Georges, it is possible to follow a much more peaceful, parallel route to the west, which runs through some famous wine villages. A similar road runs south between Pommard and Santenay.
The Côte d'Or is traditionally divided into the Côte de Nuits and the Côte de Beaune. The first, and most northern, part is named after Nuits-Saint-Georges and extends from Chenôve (a suburb of Dijon) up to and including Corgoloin. It is at this village that the Côte de Beaune begins, obviously named after Beaune which is the wine capital of Burgundy.
In general, the wines from the Côte de Nuits tend to be mainly red and somewhat sturdier than those from the Côte de Beaune. The latter district also produces all the great (and very many less great) white Burgundies. Most of the vineyards of the Côte d'Or are situated on the sunny foothills of a low, sloping mountain chain that forms a natural barrier against rain from the west.

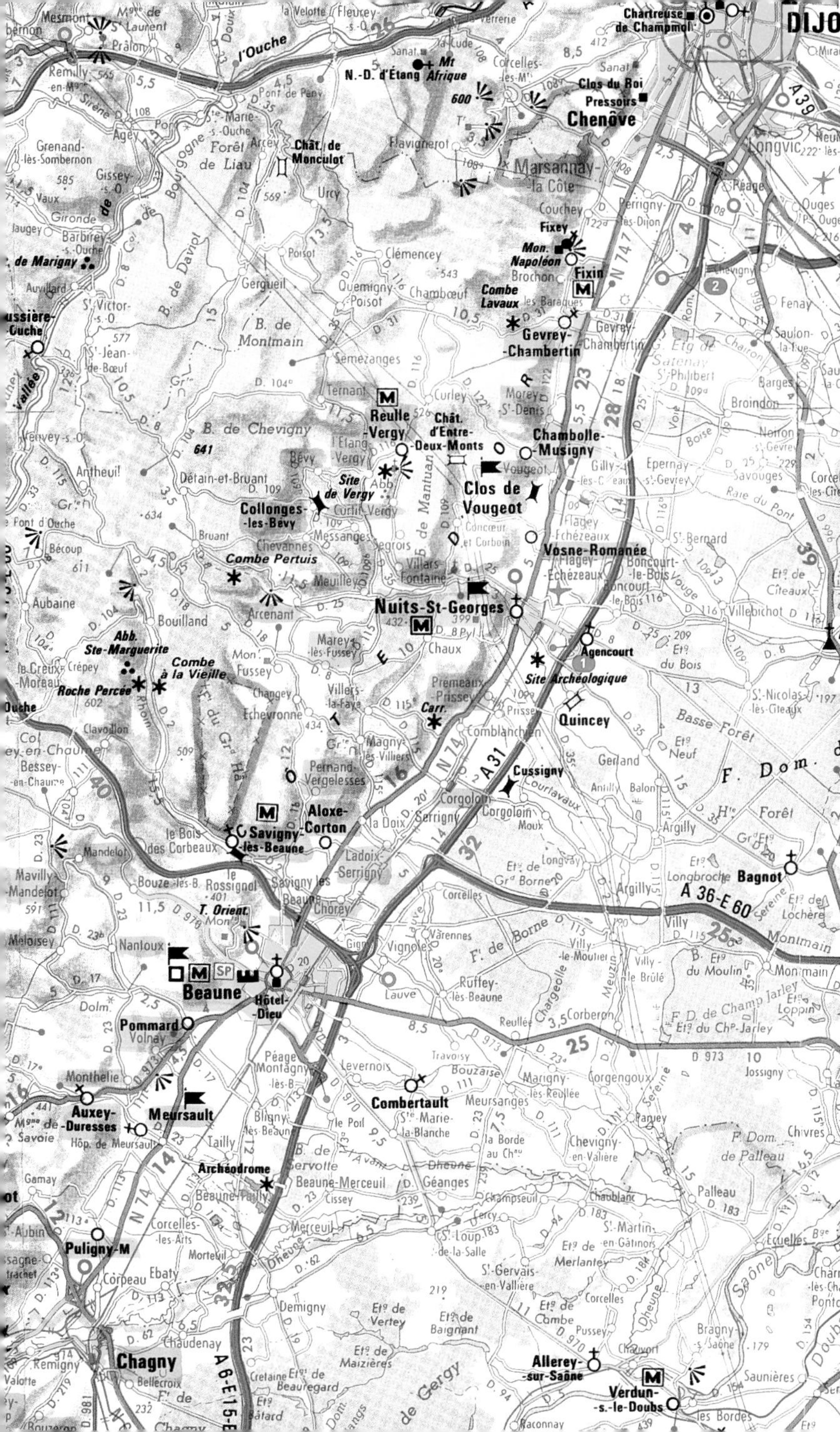

DIJO
Chartreuse de Champmol
Mesmont
Mgne de St Laurent
Prâlon
l'Ouche
la Velotte
Fleurey-s.-O.
Sanat
Mt Afrique
N.-D. d'Étang
Corcelles-les-Mts
Clos du Roi
Pressoirs
Chenôve
Remilly-en-Mgne
Pont de Pany
Ste-Marie-s.-Ouche
Agey
Grenand-lès-Sombernon
Forêt de Liau
Arcey
Chât. de Monculot
Flavignerot
Marsannay-la Côte
Longvic
Gissey-s.-O.
Urcy
Couchey
Perrigny-lès-Dijon
Ouges
Vaux
Gironde
Jaugey
Barbirey-s.-Ouche
de Marigny
Poisot
Clémencey
Fixey
Mon. Napoléon
Fixin
Brochon
Gergueil
Quemigny-Poisot
Chambœuf
Combe Lavaux
les Baraques
Gevrey-Chambertin
Fenay
Auvillard
St-Victor-s.-O.
B. de David
B. de Montmain
Semezanges
St-Jean-de-Bœuf
St-Philibert
Saulon-la-Rue
Barges
Broindon
Ternant
Reulle-Vergy
Curley
Morey-St-Denis
Chât. d'Entre-Deux-Monts
Chambolle-Musigny
B. de Chevigny
Veuvey-s.-O.
641
l'Étang-Vergy
Bévy
Site de Vergy
Vougeot
Clos de Vougeot
Gilly-lès-C.
Epernay-s.-Gevrey
Noiron-s.-Gevrey
Savouges
Corcelles-les-Cîteaux
Antheuil
Détain-et-Bruant
Collonges-les-Bévy
Curtil-Vergy
Concœur-et Corboin
Flagey-Échézeaux
Pont d'Ouche
Bruant
Messanges
Segrois
Chevannes
Bécoup
Combe Pertuis
Villars-Fontaine
Vosne-Romanée
Boncourt-le-Bois
St-Bernard
Etg de Cîteaux
Aubaine
Meuilley
Arcenant
Nuits-St-Georges
Villebichot
Bouilland
Abb. Ste-Marguerite
Marey-lès-Fussey
Chaux
Agencourt
Etg du Bois
le Creux-Moreau
Crépey
Roche Percée
Combe à la Vieille
Fussey
Premeaux-Prissey
Site Archéologique
St-Nicolas-lès-Cîteaux
Changey
Villers-la-Faye
Carr.
Prissey
Quincey
Basse Forêt
Clavoillon
Echevronne
Comblanchien
Etg Neuf
Col
Bessey-en-Chaume
Magny-lès-Villiers
Gerland
Pernand-Vergelesses
Cussigny
F. Dom.
Corgoloin
Antilly
Balon
Aloxe-Corton
la Doix
Serrigny
Moux
Argilly
Hte Forêt
le Bois des Corbeaux
Savigny-lès-Beaune
Mandelot
Ladoix-Serrigny
Longvay
Etg de Grd Borne
Longbroche
Bagnot
Mavilly-Mandelot
Bouze-lès-B.
le Rossignol
Savigny les Beaune
Chorey
Corcelles
A 36-E 60
Etg de Lochère
T. Orient.
Villy
Meloisey
Nantoux
Varennes
F. de Borne
Villy-le-Moutier
Villy-le-Brûlé
B. Etg du Moulin
Montmain
Gigny
Vignoles
Beaune
Hôtel-Dieu
Lauve
Ruffey-lès-Beaune
F. D. de Champ Jarley
Etg Loppin
Etg du Chp-Jarley
Dolm.
Pommard
Volnay
Reullée
Corberon
Péage
Montagny-lès-B.
Levernois
Travoisy
Bouzaise
Jossigny
Monthelie
Combertault
Meursanges
Marigny-lès-Reullée
Corgengoux
Auxey-Duresses
Meursault
Bligny-lès-Beaune
le Poil
Ste-Marie-la-Blanche
Pagny
Chivres
Mgne de Savoie
Hôp. de Meursault
Tailly
B. de Servotte
la Borde au Chau
Chevigny-en-Valière
F. Dom. de Palleau
Gamay
Archéodrome
Beaune-Merceuil
Géanges
Palleau
Beaune-Tailly
Cissey
Champseuil
Chaublanc
Merceuil
Cercy
St-Loup-de-la-Salle
St-Martin-en-Gâtinois
Puligny-M
Corcelles-les-Arts
Morteuil
Etg de Merlantey
Ecuelles
St-Aubin
Ebaty
St-Gervais-en-Vallière
Saône
Corpeau
Demigny
Etg de Vertey
Etg de Baignant
Etg de Combe
Corcelles
Pussey
Bragny-s.-Saône
Chaudenay
Chagny
Remigny
Etg de Maizières
Chauvort
Allerey-sur-Saône
Verdun-s.-le-Doubs
Saunières
Bellecroix
Cretaine
Etgs de Beauregard
de Gergy
les Bordes
Etg Bâtard
Naconnay
A 6-E 15-E
A 31
N 74
N 747
A 39

Dijon

The suburbs of Dijon are modern and are disfigured, above all along the *route nationale* which leads from the south into the city, with loud bill boards and ugly stores. The centre, however, is actually very fine. After a large fire in the 12th century, it was rebuilt by the Burgundian Duke Hugo II. Dijon experienced its greatest prosperity between 1364 and 1477, when four successive dukes of Valois – among them Philip the Bold – turned the city, politically and culturally, into one of the most important centres of Europe. A second flowering took place between the 16th and 18th centuries, when the princes of Condé were the governors and prosperous citizens enriched the city with marvellous buildings.

In former times, religion also played an important role. This is shown by the presence of no less than six churches in the city centre. The cathedral of Saint-Bénigne is the oldest. Its crypt and a few other parts date from the 11th century. The rest of the architecture is mainly 13th century (with 19th-century tower spires) and is in the Gothic style. One of Dijon's eight museums is situated in the former monastery buildings behind the cathedral. This is an archaeological museum. Next to the cathedral is the church of Saint-Philibert, which is Romanesque in origin.

Another striking church is the Notre-Dame, a Gothic building from the 13th century. Its wonderful façade is decorated with pseudo gargoyles and, on the tower spire to the right, the bell-ringing family of Jacquemarts, which sounds every 15 minutes. In the church there is, among other things, a Black Virgin, a wooden statue from the 12th century. The church of Saint-Michel, situated on the same square, is also worth a visit. It displays a mixture of architectural styles, among them the Flamboyant.

Walking from church to church, you are led through the most beautiful parts of the city. The rue de la Liberté is the most important shopping street and a pedestrian precinct. In this street and surrounding sidestreets are the houses of patricians, many of them half-timbered. The place François Rude is situated on the rue de la Liberté. A fountain, which is decorated with a figure treading grapes, can be found here, as well as the nicest cafés. Another street that comes out onto the place François Rude is the rue des Forges. It is full of wonderful houses from various periods and thus offers much visual pleasure. The rue de la Liberté comes out on the eastern side of the place de la Libération.

The palace of the dukes of Burgundy, now the States General of Burgundy is situated here. The façade dates from the 17th and 18th centuries. In this impressive building, the city hall and the Museum for Fine Arts are located. The museum is one of France's most important. The Musée François Rude is not far away. Here you may admire many works by the sculptor Rude, who was born in Dijon. The museum is situated in part of the former abbey of Saint-Etienne (not far from the previously mentioned church of Saint-Michel).
Having fallen under the spell of the historic riches of Dijon, you can also dine in an historic ambiance at No. 18 on the rue Sainte-Anne in the restaurant *La Toison d'Or*, which has a small museum. The collection includes wine utensils as well as model scenes, using dolls, showing high and low points from French history. You can also eat very well here (menus start at about FF 140, tel. 80.30.73.52). On the outskirts of Dijon there are also some fine things to be discovered, among

On the place François Rude there is a statue of a grape treader.

them the Jardin de l'Arquebuse, with its botanic garden, and the Museum of Natural History. There is also the Parc de la Colombière, the 17th-century creation of a pupil of Le Nôtre.

Marsannay-la-Cote

Marsannay-la-Côte was once a small wine village but, because it is located so near to Dijon, it has grown into a small commuter city with about 6000 inhabitants. As a result of constant urbanization, it has lost its vineyards.
The tiny centre is dominated by a 19th-century church which has a tower with three floors. On the church square you can quench your thirst in two bars, *Café de la Place,* owned by Christian Bouvier, and *Café des Sports* or 'Chez Marianne'. Here, and in the local restaurants, the most famous rosé of Burgundy is served, Rosé de Marsannay. It was made for the first time on September 23 by the brilliant winegrower Joseph Clair. He did not use the much-planted gamay but the noble pinot noir. The wine became an enormous success and the rosé developed into the speciality of Marsannay. The village still makes rosé nowadays, but the accent is really on red wine, which accounts for three times the volume of rosé. Since 1987, the rosé, the red wine and tiny amounts of white wine bear the *appellation* Marsannay. This *appellation* is also

Restaurants
Les Gourmets
✆ 80.52.16.32
Celebrated, busy restaurant where the quality of the food is high and the style of cooking rather classical and with a light touch. You will find many modern creations on the menu, such as *osso bucco* or chicken with cider vinegar. Apart from numerous regional wines, the wine list also contains good local wines. The interior is modern. The garden and terrace are not visible from the street. Menus start at about FF 175.

Gourmets will really enjoy themselves in Les Gourmets.

Recommended Producers

Domaine André Bart The wines of this average-sized estate vary in quality. By far the best are the grands crus Bonnes Mares and Chambertin Clos de Bèze.

Marc Brocot Strikingly good red Marsannay, originating from old vines.

Domaine Philippe Charlopin-Parizot Most of the wines from this medium-sized producer are above average quality. This is particularly true of the Clos Saint-Denis, the ordinary Morey-Saint-Denis and the Charmes-Chambertin.

Bruno Clair His Rosé de Marsannay is absolutely delicious and his traditionally vinified red wines – such as Savigny-lès-

Marsannay is dominated by its church.

La Renardière
✆ 80.52.16.41
Simple eating-house where *coq au vin, rognon de veau à l'ancienne* and similar dishes are served on tables decked out in pink linen. Various meals under FF 100.

used in the neighbouring districts of Chenôve (in the north) and Couchey (in the south).
One place of interest in the hilly wine village of Chenôve is the Pressoir des Ducs, a formidable winepress from 1228. Couchey has a fine church with a many-coloured spire.

Beaune La Dominode, various premiers crus from Gevrey-Chambertin, Chambertin Clos de Bèze and Marsannay La Casse Tête – draw admiration. Also white wines, among them the rare white Fixin and Morey-Saint-Denis.
Albert Derey (Couchey) Rents a tiny vineyard of less than half a hectare, named Clos des Marc d'Or, from the city of Dijon. It is planted with chardonnay, which gives a generous, pleasant wine with a certain distinction.
Domaine Huguenot Père & Fils
Decent, dark Burgundies, often marked by wood. They also have a pleasant Rosé de Marsannay.

The old bread oven of Fixey.

Fixin

In Fixin, formerly called Fiscentix, the dukes of Burgundy had a summer residence. The 12th-century building was later given to the monks of Cîteaux, who turned it into a sanitorium. The building still exists and now belongs to the wine estate, Clos de la Perrière. Fixin and the neighbouring hamlet of Fixey have beautiful churches with multicoloured tower spires. In Fixey there is also an old bread oven which has been entirely restored. It is in the street leading to the church and the hotel. These places of interest are overlooked by the Parc Noisot, which is situated beside a wooded hill above Fixin. It was created in 1837 by Claude Noisot, an old commandant of the imperial guard, and was intended to honour Napolean. A solid replica of the house in which the

Hotel

Domaine de Saint-Antoine Fixey
✆ 80.52.46.16
Very peacefully situated countryside hotel, located in an old building. Six, somewhat rustic, rooms offer adequate comfort. Prices about FF 300. There is a view of the village from the hotel car park.

Restaurants

Chez Jeanette
✆ 80.52.45.49
This is the best known of four local restaurants. The interior of this inn is rural in character and numerous Burgundian specialities appear on the menu. Below FF 150 there is a choice of three menus. It is also a simple hotel.

'Réveil de Napoléon' in the Parc Noisot.

Recommended Producers

Vincent et Denis Berthaut The robust, solid wines of this estate are made traditionally and usually require at least a decade of patience. The best are Fixin Les Arvelets, Fixin Les Clos and Fixin Les Cras.

Jacques Durand-Roblot A winegrower who is rather conservative in his methods and whose somewhat rustic, reliable Fixin and Gevrey-Chambertin are frequently sold to private individuals.

Domaine Pierre Gelin A prominent local name. The red wines are absolutely reliable, among them the Fixin Clos du Chapitre, Fixin Clos Napoléon, Fixin Les Hervelets, Fixin and two grands crus,

Fixin's church tower has a multicoloured spire.

exiled emperor lived on St. Helena was built in the park; in the small stone building all sorts of mementoes of Napoleon were gathered together. Two bronze statues are found elsewhere in the park, the Reveil de Napoléon (as he 'awakes to immortality') and the bust of artist François Rude who made the statue. The park was bequeathed to the municipality of Fixin by Claude Noiset and attracts thousands of visitors. Napoleon's name is also found in many other spots in Fixin. There is a vineyard Clos Napoléon. Fixin's wines, which are mainly red, are usually sturdy in constitution and can undergo bottle ripening without problems.

La Petite Taverne
✆ 80.52.45.56
This establishment, situated on a street corner, offers mainly regional dishes which are prepared with care. The *coq à la lie de vin* is excellent. Menus start at about FF 80.

Tourist Tips

In the direction of Gevrey-Chambertin, you will pass a temple-like spa dating from 1827. The water comes from an old well, is rich in iron and good for digestive problems.

Chambertin Clos de Bèze and Mazis-Chambertin.

Philippe Joliet The building on this estate was constructed by monks and has fabulous cellars and an antique press. Only one wine is made, Fixin Clos de la Perrière. It is a powerful red Burgundy with a warm, generous taste and an excellent ageing potential.

Related to Wine

In the 17th-century cellar of Domaine du Clos Saint-Louis, situated in neighbouring Fixey, a small museum displaying wine utensils has been established.

Gevrey-Chambertin

Directly to the south of the village of Gevrey-Chambertin, a series of grand cru vineyards extend to the right and left of the D 122. Clos de Bèze was the first field (7th century) to be planted with grapevines. A farmer called Bertin, later planted vines on the plot of land next to it: *le champ de Bertin*, which has been corrupted to Le Chambertin. The wines from here enjoyed just as good a name as those of the Clos de Bèze, therefore the vineyard gradually came to be called Chambertin Clos de Bèze. The wines of Le Chambertin became famous in the time of Napoleon, who drank them at each meal and also during battles. The village of Gevrey added Chambertin to its

The church of Saint-Aignan.

Near the northern entry to the village.

Hotel

Les Grands Crus
✆ 80.34.34.15
Peacefully situated; 24 rooms (starting at FF 300), some of which have a view of a vineyard and the castle. The beds are not all that large and the interior is rather boring. The big lobby, with its fireplace, is cosier.

Restaurants

Les Millésimes
✆ 80.51.84.24
At walking distance from *Les Grands Crus*. Situated in a tastefully furnished vaulted cellar. The cooking here is inventive and of high quality. Wine cellar with about 45,000 bottles. Menus start at FF 300. There are plans for a

The Les Millésimes restaurant.

Recommended Producers

Domaine Bachelet Minute property.
Pierre Bourée Fils Small wine merchant.
Camus Père & Fils Rather large estate with a brilliant portfolio of land.
Domaine Pierre Damoy About 5.3 ha. Chambertin Clos de Bèze.
Domaine Drouhin-Laroze Distinguished wine estate.
Frédéric Humbert Reliable.
Naigeon-Chauveau/Domaine des Varoilles Small, reliable wine merchant.
Domaine Pernot-Fourrier Emphasis is on quality.
Domaine Les Perrières Limited produc-

The famous Chambertin Clos de Bèze grand cru.

name in 1847. The same coupling is also found in the other grands crus, Chapelle-Chambertin, Charmes-Chambertin (by far the largest), Griotte-Chambertin, Latricières-Chambertin, Mazis-Chambertin (also spelt Mazys and Mazi) and Ruchottes-Chambertin. As a village, Gevrey-Chambertin is larger and more extensive than most of the other communities of Côte d'Or. A castle with angular towers and wine cellars, the church of Saint-Aignan and the Clos du Chapitre (13th-century cellars) are worth seeing. The wines of *Brochon*, to the north, may also be sold as Gevrey-Chambertin. Brochon has a Neo-Renaissance castle (cannot be visited), formerly owned by the poet Stephen Liégeard, who made his own wine in the 1920s.

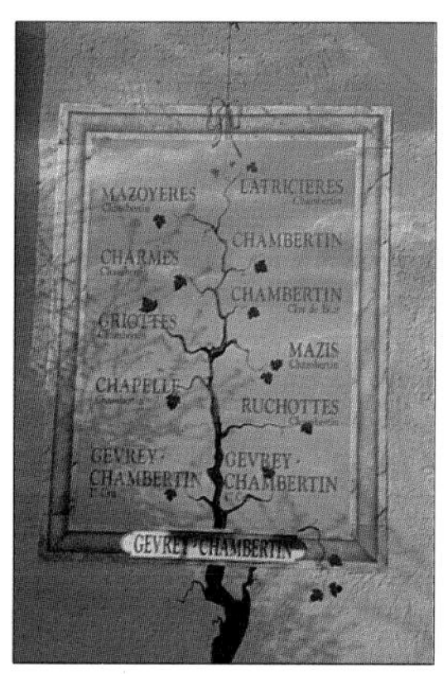

Wall painting in the centre.

four-star hotel with 30 rooms.

La Rôtisserie du Chambertin
✆ 80.34.33.20
You enter this stylish cellar restaurant by way of a small museum. Refined regional cuisine. Sublime *coq au vin.* There is usually *fricassée de grenouilles et d'escargots.* Menus start at FF 300.

La Sommellerie
✆ 80.34.31.48
In the village centre. Specialises in regional dishes (*blanc de poulet à la moutarde, coq au vin*). Lunch menu including wine about FF 100. Other menus start at about FF 150.

Tourist Tips

In Brochon, just to the north of Gevrey-Chambertin, there is a small amusement park: Florida Park. Various attractions, among them a roller-coaster and a miniature train. It can be reached by means of the *route nationale.*

tion from this small producer.
Joseph Roty Impressive winegrower who is a real perfectionist.
Domaine Armand Rousseau Père & Fils High-class wines.
Also Recommended Philippe Batacchi, Lucien Boillot & Fils, Alain Burguet, Michel Cluny & Fils, Dom. Esmonin Père & Fils, Geantet-Pansiot, Laurent Goillot-Bernollin, Philippe Leclerc, Dom. René Leclerc, Henri Magnien & Fils, Dom. Maume, Philippe Rossignol, Dom. Roy Père & Fils, Dom. Tortochot.

HOTEL

Castel de Très Girard

✆ 80.34.33.09

This three-star hotel is situated within earshot of the *route nationale*, but, because the hotel lies at right angles to the road, the noise is bearable. The rooms have character and space and are furnished with all conveniences. Prices start at about FF 250. Outdoor swimming pool. The restaurant offers good food. Apart from regional specialities it also serves modern dishes. Menus start at about FF 200, plus a less expensive weekday lunch menu.

TOURIST TIPS

- Morey-Saint-Denis comprises a small, upper section (which you enter from Gevrey-Chambertin), a middle section (the largest) and a low-lying suburb (on the other side of the *route nationale*). You will find wine cellars in all three of the sections.
- Visitors to the Clos de Tart will see some excellently preserved presses from the 12th century.

MOREY-SAINT-DENIS

Cellar wall of the Clos de Tart.

When you enter the village of Morey-Saint-Denis by way of the *route nationale*, you immediately encounter the cellars of the grand cru Clos de Tart. This vineyard (about 7.5 hectares.) has always been the property of a single owner – since 1932 this has been the wine estate of Mommessin. The grand cru to which Morey-Saint-Denis owes the second half of its name (the first part probably means a Moorish estate or field) is Clos Saint-Denis, which

Part of Bonnes Mares is situated in Morey-Saint-Denis.

RECOMMENDED PRODUCERS

Bryczek Père & Fils Colourful cellar.
Domaine Dujac Refined wines.
Domaine des Lambrays Owner of the Clos des Lambrays.
Hubert Lignier Marvellous Burgundies.
J. Taupenot-Merme Delicious wines.
J. Truchot-Martin Works classically.

Also Recommended Dom. Pierre Amiot & Fils, Dom. Arlaud Père & Fils, Domaine Robert Gibourg, Dom. Robert Groffier, Georges Lignier & Fils, Michel Magnien, Henri Perrot-Minot, Dom. Ponsot, Dom. Jean Raphet, Dom. B. Serveau & Fils, Clos de Tart.

The village street; to the left is the church.

produces firm but soft wines. Clos des Lambrays lies between Clos de Tart and Clos Saint-Denis. It is a rather young grand cru (1981) and is also, for the most part, in the hands of a single owner. To the north of Clos Saint-Denis is Clos de la Roche, which borders on Gevrey-Chambertin. It is the most famous, and the largest, local grand cru and gives the strongest wines of the district. Tasted blindfolded, they are very much like those of the grands crus of Gevrey-Chambertin. Besides power, a good Clos de la Roche also has a certain elegance, plus a touch of fruit (above all wild cherries) and sometimes a touch of violets. The remaining wines of Morey-Saint-Denis usually taste less robust, without being light. Except for the 18th-century church, the village has few places of interest.

In the cellar of Bryczek Père & Fils.

- The inhabitants of Morey-Saint-Denis were nicknamed 'the wolves' centuries ago because they were abandoned by their rulers and had to scavenge in order to live.

Castel de Très Girard, a good place to stay.

Related to Wine

- In Nuits-Saints-Georges,on the Sunday before Palm Sunday, the auction of the Hospices de Nuits takes place. On the Friday before, the wines of Morey-Saint-Denis can be tasted. The event is called Le Carrefour de Dionysos.
- A small part of the grand cru Bonnes Mares is situated within the municipality of Morey-Saint-Denis (see Chambolle-Musigny).

Chambolle-Musigny

Until late in the 1980s there wasn't much to be seen in Chambolle-Musigny except the late-Gothic village church (with its striking tower and marvellous, rediscovered 16th-century frescos). This changed when the Swiss wine estate of André Ziltener renovated one of the local castles and renamed it Château André Ziltener. The 18th-century building is now a luxurious apartment-hotel. The cellars have been turned into a museum which is open seven days a week and also during lunchtime. It also functions as a sales area for the rather costly wines of Ziltener. A little further on is the Château de Chambolle-Musigny (not open to visitors), which is at the heart of a small wine estate. The light,

Hotel
Château André Ziltener
© 80.62.81.37
After the spring of 1993 this castle will have over 10 luxurious apartments, with marble bathrooms and a lot of privacy. The prices are aimed at a well-to-do clientele.

Château de Chambolle-Musigny.

Restaurant
Le Chambolle-Musigny
© 80.62.86.26
Small restaurant, entirely renovated in 1992, which, at reasonable prices, serves Burgundian specialities – and a lot of local wines.

The luxurious Château André Ziltener hotel.

Recommended Producers

Domaine Bertheau Traditional.

Daniel Moine-Hudelot Wines full of character are produced from the various small plots of land, including Musigny.

Domaine Jacques-Frédéric Mugnier This modest wine estate is situated in the Château de Chambolle-Musigny. It produces, among others, a sublime Musigny.

Domaine G. Roumier This is the home of fantastic, aromatic Burgundies which, in their category, are as good as is possible. It is a privilege to taste the masterful Musigny, the variegated Clos Vougeot, the sometimes almost opulent Bonnes Mares and the excellent Ruchottes-

The village is situated in a small valley.

lime-bearing soil gives the red wines of Chambolle-Musigny the finest structure of the entire Côte de Nuits. They are charming, full of subtlety – but at the same time strong enough to ripen excellently in the bottle. The very best of the best that is produced by this municipality comes from the grand cru Le Musigny. Its wine is described by Gaston Roupnel as 'from silk and from lace'. The other grand cru, Bonnes Mares (a small part of which lies within Morey-Saint-Denis), gives a somewhat soft wine, less delicate but still delicious. Feminine grace and delicacy are just as strongly present in the wines of premiers crus, such as Amoureuses and Charmes – which rightfully bear these names.

Diorama in Château André Ziltener.

Gable coat of arms with wine symbol.

Tourist Tips

In the hills behind Chambolle-Musigny a ravine begins, which later splits in two. Above the fork, on a wooded rock, there is a charming little chapel.

Chambertin, while the Chambolle-Musigny Amoureuses is almost on the level of a grand cru.

Hervé Roumier Passionate, thoroughly schooled winegrower.

Domaine Comte Georges de Vogüé This is one of the great names of Burgundy, thanks, in part, to his ownership of about 7 hectares out of the almost 11 that the grand cru Musigny accounts for. At their best the Musignies – the Cuvée Vieilles Vignes and the ordinary – reach the height of finesse.

Also Recommended Gaston Barthod-Noëllat, Servelle-Tachot, Ziltener.

HOTELS

Domaine Bertagna
✆ 80.62.86.04
This wine estate has more than a dozen rooms around a courtyard. Very comfortable, with shower and toilet. Choice of a large or small breakfast. Prices start at about FF 300.

Château de Gilly
Gilly-lès-Cîteaux
✆ 80.62.89.98
This marvellous Cistercian castle dates from the 14th century and is, at present, a luxurious hotel with a tennis court and a park. Prices start

VOUGEOT

The village of Vougeot consists of not much more than an 800-metre-long street with a few short side streets. The reason that it attracts tens of thousands of visitors annually is the austere, 16th-century castle, Château de Vougeot, which is situated in the middle of a large, walled vineyard a few hundred metres from the village centre. The castle was built by the monks of Cîteaux and, since 1944, has been the property of Les Chevaliers du Tastevin. This wine fraternity holds its initiations, festive dinners and tasting sessions here, while the castle also functions as a wine museum. In the museum are four enormous winepresses from the time of the monks.

The Clos Vougeot, as seen from the route nationale.

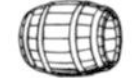

RECOMMENDED PRODUCERS

Domaine Bertagna The German winegrowing family of Reh has extended this wine estate since 1982 and has also much improved the quality of the wines. Half the volume of the Burgundies, matured in oak from the Vosges, is sold locally. Among the specialities are Clos Vougeot, white Vougeot and red Vougeot Clos de la Perrière.

Georges Clerget Small wine property which makes well-constructed, aromatic wines, including Vougeot premier cru and Echézeaux.

Michel Clerget Minimal production, with, among others, a fine Chambolle-

Ten men were often needed to work one of the presses. The surrounding vineyard, Clos Vougeot, is about 50 hectares and is the property of around 70 different owners who produce extremely varying wines. The Clos Vougeot is actually a miniature Burgundy, because nowhere else is it so completely true that the reputation of a producer is a more important selection criterion than the name or status of the vineyard. Furthermore, the largest landowner of this grand cru is Château de la Tour; the building of the same name is a mini-castle which was built on the edge of the vineyard in 1890. Next to the Clos Vougeot, near the entrance to Château de Vougeot, is a vineyard where a cordial white wine is made, Clos Blanc de Vougeot.

Castle dinner of Les Chevaliers du Tastevin.

Domaine Bertagna, which is also a hotel.

at FF 600. In the cellar restaurant the cooking is very good (menus start at about FF 200).

RESTAURANT
Aux Gastronomes
✆ 80.62.85.10
Relatively trustworthy place to dine with very conventional dishes on the one hand (*entrecôte grillée*) and, on the other hand, some rather more inventive ones. The least inexpensive menu costs about FF 100.

Musigny Charmes.
Alain Hudelot-Noëllat Average-sized estate where the wines are vinified with more than ordinary care. Most of them have a formidable quality, such as Clos Vougeot, Romanée-St. Vivant, Richebourg and various premiers crus from Vosne-Romanée.
Bernard Munier (Gilly-lès-Cîteaux) Producer of elegant, pleasant red wines, including a Chambolle-Musigny.
Château de la Tour With 5.4 hectares, this is the largest landowner of the Clos de Vougeot. Despite a few improvements, the only wine, Clos Vougeot, is not really great.

Strikingly painted restaurant.

Restaurants

Losset

✆ 80.62.88.10

This eating-house leads an inconspicous existence in the hardly exciting Flagey-Echézeaux. It is situated next to the church and on the façade is written 'Bar Tabac'. However, many winegrowers and their guests know where to find it, above all around noon, because you can eat excellent, generously portioned, inexpensive dishes here.

Vosne-Romanee

Nobody would visit Vosne-Romanée because of its architectural beauty (one 16th-century residence plus a castle without much allure). The wine though, is another story. There are seven grands crus within this district. A few of them are legendary. The place of honour is taken by La Romanée-Conti, a field which can be recognized by a high stone cross with an inscription on the base. The present owner is the Domaine de la Romanée-Conti, in existence since 1942, in which the families Leroy and De Villaine have equal ownership. The red wine, La Romanée-Conti, has the same unique position within Bur-

Recommended Producers

Robert Arnoux Beautiful, broad wines.
Coquard-Loison-Fleurot In Flagey-Echézeaux.
Jean Grivot A family estate where wines of high to very high quality are made.
Domaine Jean Gros Top estate.
Domaine Lamarche Including La Grande Rue.
Domaine Leroy Concentrated nectars which can ripen for decades without problems.
Domaine Méo-Camuzet Elegant wines.
Gérard et René Mugneret Very reliable.
A. Pernin-Rossin Well-constructed wines.

The cross of La Romanée-Conti.

gundy as the white wine Le Montrachet: there is none better. La Romanée-Conti is a well-nigh perfect wine with a special finesse, a large abundance of gradations and perfect balance. It requires at least ten years of patience and then tastes both luxurious and satiny. Another famous grand cru is La Tâche, likewise the sole property of the Domaine de la Romanée-Conti. This wine is generally somewhat earthier than that of La Romanée-Conti, with a marvellous broad taste (spices, mushrooms, red fruits and berries, freshly mown grasses). The other grands crus are: Le Richebourg (overwhelming, yet complex wines), La Romanée-St. Vivant (elegant), the small La Romanée (strong, colourful wines), La Grande Rue (firm and fine) and two fields which actually belong to Flagey-Echézeaux – Grands Echézeaux and Echézeaux. The first gives the best wines, aromatic, civilized and lightly spiced.

La Toute Petite Auberge
✆ 80.61.02.03
Apparently in order to draw attention to his business – it is situated next to the *route nationale* – the owner has painted this building bright red. The menus (starting at FF 75) offer regional dishes such as *boeuf bourguignon, filet de boeuf et sa petite sauce au vin, coq au vin* and the like. These are prepared with care.

Vosne-Romanée is surrounded by vineyards.

Domaine de la Romanée-Conti No wine estate is as famous as this one – with corresponding prices. The two families that run it are the sole owners of La Romanée-Conti and La Tâche, two grands crus that give brilliant wines. Other celebrities are Romanée-St. Vivant, Richebourg and the white Montrachet.

Robert Sirugue Average-sized estate.
Also Recommended Jacques Cacheux-Blée & Fils, Dom. René Engel, Dom. Forey Père & Fils, Dom. François Gerbet, Henri Jayer/Emmanuel Rouget, Mongeard-Mugneret, Georges Mugneret/A. Mugneret-Gibourg, Dom. Robert Noblet.

Hotel

La Gentilhommière
✆ 80.61.12.06
A few kilometres west of Nuits, on the D 25. Nice, peaceful rooms (20) start at about FF 350. The restaurant is furnished in rural chic. Regional dishes prepared with care. Menus start at FF 180.

Restaurants

Caveau Saint-Ugezon
✆ 80.61.21.59
Near the *beffroi*, next to a large cheese store (the same owner). Very inexpensive menus, tasty salads, cheese platters and reasonably priced wines. Nice place for lunch.

La Côte d'Or
✆ 80.61.06.10
Refined cuisine. Pleasurable ambiance. Menu through the week

Various 'open' cellars.

Nuits-Saint-Georges

Nuits-Saint-Georges has been called the 'kidney of Burgundy', because a huge number of wine taverns are situated here, including a few very large ones. As well as wine, much traffic also flows through the capital of Côte de Nuits: the *route nationale* runs close to the centre, with tasting and sales premises on both sides. The heart of Nuits is the place de la République, which is surrounded by shops. It has a 17th-century clock tower (*beffroi*) in which the archaeological museum is situated (with finds from excavations in Les Bolards). On the west side of the city is the most beautiful church of the Côte de Nuits, the Romanesque Saint-Symphorien. On the south side of Nuits is the Hospice Saint-Laurent. This 17th-century hospital has a remarkable statue of the Virgin Mary. Just as in Beaune, the hospitals of Nuits have been given wine land and their wines are auctioned two weeks before Easter. They are mainly premiers

In the city centre.

Recommended Producers

Jean Claude Boisset One of the largest firms of the Côte d'Or. Owner of, among others, Lionel J. Bruck, Jaffelin, Pierre Ponnelle and Charles Viénot.
F. Chauvenet Important wine merchant.
Jean Chauvenet Excellent producer.
Dufouleur Père & Fils Wine merchant, specializing in rather robust wines.
Joseph Faiveley Belongs to the foremost group of Burgundy merchants.
Geisweiler & Fils Since 1988 it has been the property of the German Reh family.
Labouré-Roi Quality firm.
Moillard A large wine merchant, which

crus from Nuits-Saint-Georges itself and their average quality is high. One of the best known, and also best, vineyards is Les Saint-Georges, a premier cru – grands crus do not exist here. Wines of equal quality come from the premiers crus Les Vaucrains, Les Pruliers and Les Porrets. All of these fields are situated on the south side of the city. A characteristic Nuits-Saint-Georges is a colourful red Burgundy with a muscular taste, in which some tannin is present. Lighter types are also made, which are charming after a few years, having a fruity suppleness. A small amount of white grapes is harvested here, from which, among others, a luxuriant white La Perrière is made. The *appellation* Nuits-Saint-Georges also extends to the southern, neighbouring district of Prémeaux (see the following section).

Peace is assured in La Gentilhommière.

from about FF 150, ordinary menu starting at about FF 270. Extensive wine list. Also a hotel.

Le Sanglier
✆ 80.61.04.79
Rural inn on the D 25, not far past La Gentilhommière. Inexpensive menus and meat dishes from the grill. When the weather is good, lunch is served outside.

Tourist Tips

- In order to visit the Gallic-Roman excavation of Les Bolards follow the road to Seurre from Nuits. After an industrial zone, look for a small signpost at a turning.
- From Nuits it is only 11 kilometers to the abbey of Cîteaux. The monks make delicious cheese.

The Hospice Saint-Laurent.

is technically very well equipped.
Also Recommended Marcel Bocquenet, Dom. Henri Gouges, Alain Michelot, Dom. Henri Remoriquet.

Related to Wine
Near the northern entrance of Nuits-Saint-Georges, Le Berchère is situated. This is one of the most impressive local locations for tasting. In cellars dating from the beginning of the 19th century, there are about 1000 casks and 600,000 bottles. Usually around 20 wines, arranged by theme, can be tasted here. The establishment is the property of the Moillard firm.

Hotel

Hôtel Le Manassès
Curtil-Vergy
✆ 80.61.43.81
This hotel has seven rooms and is very peacefully situated. It was opened in 1991. The rooms are neat, with modern comfort and a somewhat rustic ambiance. All guests are offered a free wine tasting session.

Restaurants

Auberge la Ruelée
✆ 80.61.44.11
Rural inn, within walking distance of the local hotel. Very inexpensive, weekday lunch menu and ordinary menus starting at about FF 100. Regional cuisine. There is a small terrace at the rear.

Hautes-Cotes de Nuits

To the west of Nuits-Saint-Georges lies the district of Hautes-Côtes de Nuits. The Burgundies here generally have less depth than those from Côte de Nuits but also cost far less. The white wines (including Bourgogne Aligoté) are usually of the highest quality. From the point of view of a tourist, Hautes-Côtes de Nuits is just as interesting as Côte de Nuits. The landscape is extremely varied. Some of the nicest villages are situated along the following route. By taking the D 25 from the direction of Nuits-Saint-Georges, and then taking the D 35 after the restaurant *Le Sanglier*, you pass the steep vineyard (Les Genièvres) of small *Villars-Fontaine* with its modest little castle. A pretty road

The church of Reulle-Vergy.

The Maison des Hautes-Côtes in Marey-lès-Fussey.

Recommended Producers

Yves Chaley/Domaine du Val de Vergy (Curtil-Vergy) Stainless steel is used here and a cooling system regulates the fermentation temperature. Pure, delicious wines are the result. Old wine utensils are on display in one room and wine is tasted among these museum pieces. The Chaley family also runs a hotel.

Domaine Bernard Hudelot-Verdel (Villars-Fontaine) The owner is one of the pioneers of Hautes-Côtes. Charming white Burgundy Hautes-Côtes de Nuits and a red wine marked by wood.

Jayer-Gilles (Magny-lès-Villers) Exemplary red wines which belong to the top of

now leads to *Curtil-Vergy* (with the ruins of a 9th-century monastery). Drive to *Reulle-Vergy*, with its regional museum, old bathing place and the 13th-century church of Saint-Saturnin situated above the village. Follow the road to *Ternant*. Past this village, in the direction of *Rolle*, two dolmen can be seen in the middle of a forest (close to the road). Rolle has a nice restaurant. Go back to *l'Etang-Vergy* by way of Ternant. The overgrown walls of the old castle can best be seen by driving in the direction of *Bévy* and then looking back. The church tower in Bévy has a copper dome. A lovely road runs from Bévy to *Collonges-lès-Bévy*, with its 17th-century castle. After this comes *Chevannes*, which has a little, old church with a multicoloured spire. Now go on to *Arcenant* by way of Meuilly. Apart from wine, liqueur is also made here. Travel further southwards to *Marey-lès-Fussey* with its Romanesque church and the *Maison des Hautes-Côtes* restaurant (beautiful view).

Honey sale in Arcenant.

Ferme de Rolle
Hameau de Rolle
(near Ternant)
✆ 80.61.40.10
Cosy eating-house situated in an old farm. Regional cuisine. The façade is decorated with a red apple.

Maison des Hautes-Côtes
Marey-lès-Fussey
✆ 80.62.91.29
Regional wines and pure Burgundian dishes are served here. Three menus, costing less than FF 100.

Ternant is beautifully situated.

In Curtil-Vergy.

their category. Most of the red wines age in new oak casks. Echézeaux, Côte de Nuits-Villages, red Bourgogne Hautes-Côtes de Nuits, etc.
Henri Naudin-Ferran (Magny-lès-Villers) Very fine white Hautes Côtes de Nuits.
Domaine Thévenot-Le-Brun & Fils (Marey-lès-Fussey) With 25 hectares, one of the largest properties.
Alain Verdet (Arcenant) Often crowned.
Also Recommended Claude Cornu (Magny-lès-Villers), Domaine Marcel et Bernard Fribourg (Villers-la-Faye), Simon Fils (Marey-lès-Fussey).

Restaurants

Auberge de la Miotte
Ladoix-Serrigny
✆ 80.26.40.75
A former, 18th-century hunting lodge behind the church of Serrigny. In the rustic dining room, *coq au vin, boeuf bourguignon, cuisse de canard au baies de cassis* and other inexpensive regional dishes are served (menus start at about FF 75).

Between Nuits and Aloxe

The almost 10-kilometre-long *route nationale* between Nuits-Saint-Georges and the exit to Aloxe-Corton runs, for a large part, past ribbon development. Only the first section, between Nuits and Prémeaux-Prissey, is surrounded by vineyards. It is worth turning left in *Prémeaux* in order to see the lovely little church with its multi-coloured roof. By driving downwards and keeping to the right, you will pass the Château de Prémeaux, where a small wine estate is located. Prémeaux-Prissey runs seamlessly into Comblanchien, which borders on Corgoloin. In both districts stone pits and brickyards are situated beside the road. The pink, marble-like stone of Comblanchien was used, among other things, for the Opéra in Paris. *Corgoloin*, with its 13th-century church, is situated on the border between Côte de Nuits and Côte de Beaune. It is indicated by a sign near the Clos des Langres, which is a walled vineyard. In the marvellous cellars of the Clos des Langres, built by Cistercian

Clos des Langres, where a fine press stands.

Les Coquines
Ladoix-Serrigny
(Buisson)
✆ 80.26.43.58
On the *route nationale*. This is a very good place to eat, where the cooking is inventive and much attention has

Recommended Producers

Prémeaux-Prissey

Domaine Bertrand Ambroise Small estate, delicious great wines.

Robert Dubois & Fils Dynamic, well-schooled, progressive winegrowing family.

Domaine Machard de Gramont Large property with land in Côte de Nuits as well as in Côte de Beaune.

Domaine Daniel Rion & Fils Modern, well equipped estate along the *route nationale*. Clear-tasting wines, with wood, juiciness and often an aroma of red berries and fruits. Nuits-Saint-Georges and Vosne-Romanée are excellently

The small church of Prémeaux.

been given to the interior. Menus start at around FF 125.

Tourist Tips

After having been closed for years, the Clos de Langres in Corgoloin is now open to visitors. The estate is run by La Reine Pédauque from Aloxe-Corton and produces a good Côte de Nuits-Villages.

monks, is a magnificent press from the 18th century. After Corgoloin comes *Ladoix-Serrigny*, a commuter village which has a nice little castle (cannot be visited) and, near the exit to Aloxe-Corton, the chapel of Notre-Dame de la Chemin (11th and 15th centuries).
The wines of Prémeaux are sold as Nuits-Saint-Georges, those of Prissey, Comblanchien and Cor goloin as Côte de Nuits-Villages, those of Ladoix-Serrigny as Ladoix, Côte de Beaune-Villages and, in part, as Aloxe-Corton premier cru plus Corton.

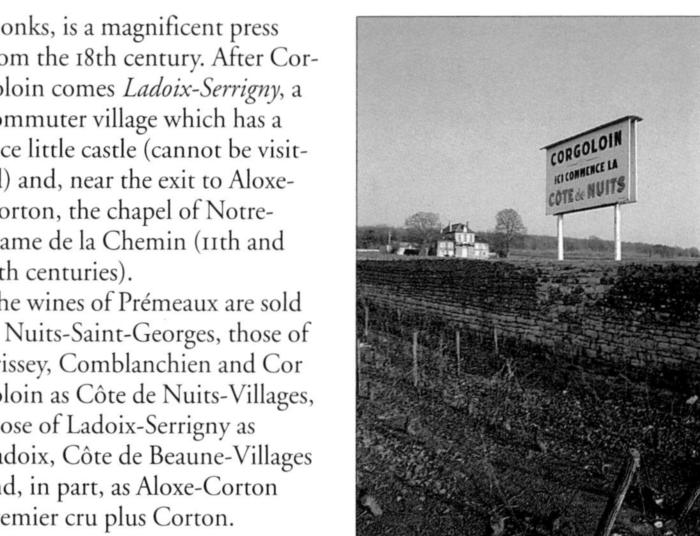

The border of the 'Côtes'.

represented by premiers crus.
Also Recommended: Dom. des Perdrix.
Ladoix-Serrigny
Capitain-Gagnerot Reliable wines, with Corton-Charlemagne and Corton Les Renardes as its stars. The Ladoix La Micaude is also worth discovering.
Chevalier Père & Fils Hospitable wine-growing family (they live in Buisson).
Prince Florent de Mérode Strong Cortons of high quality.
Domaine André Nudant & Fils Rather large property with good white and red wines.

HOTEL
Hôtel Clarion
✆ 80.26.46.70
Close to the Château Corton-André, the Voarick family has built a small, 10-room hotel which is furnished with great taste. Every room is different but offers the same comfort. Prices start at about FF 450.

ALOXE-CORTON

Charlemagne was crazy about the red wines from Aloxe but often spilled them on his white beard. His mother, Berthe au Grand Pied (who had one foot larger than the other), complained so much about the red stains that Charlemagne ordered that the vineyard be replanted with white grapes. This was done but a great wine was not the result. The grape variety planted was the simple aligoté and it was not until the last century that the more noble chardonnay replaced it.
A great white wine was then born. It has a broad taste and a full, rich aroma in which both ripe fruit and wood are present, as well as a touch of

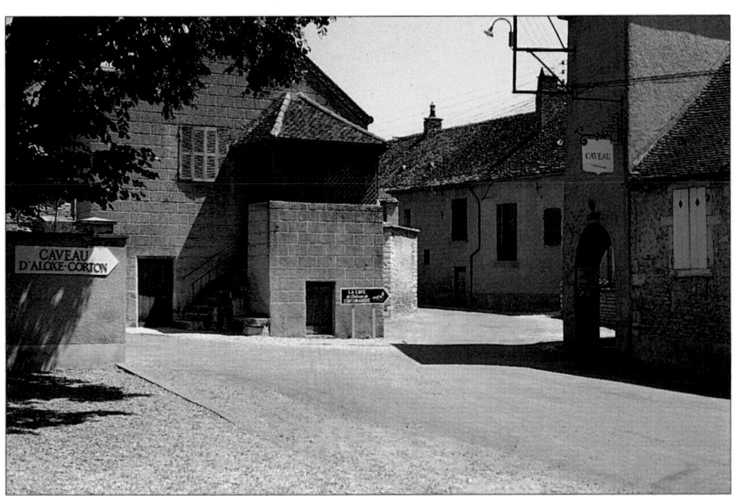

Village square with a collective tasting room to the right.

RECOMMENDED PRODUCERS
Caves de la Reine Pédauque With the help of a sister firm, Pierre André, this large wine merchant became the owner of Château Corton-André (bought in 1927). In general, the wines from their own land (in both Burgundy and the Rhône Valley) are the best, followed closely by a few superior *cuvées* (such as the Dominière selection).
Domaine Daniel Senard An average-sized estate with exemplary red wines, including four Cortons (such as the Clos des Meix) and a rare white Aloxe-Corton which reminds one of a minor Corton-Charlemagne.

honey and cinnamon. In honour of Charlemagne, it was called Corton-Charlemagne. The vineyard of the same name, a grand cru, is situated on the southeast slope of the Corton hill, the wooded crown of which rises high above Aloxe-Corton. The other slopes produce red Corton, likewise a formidable wine. At its best, it tastes generous and firm, while retaining style and distinction. The compactly built Aloxe-Corton has a fine 15th-century castle, Château Corton-André, which has a multicoloured roof and is the property of a business firm. The castle, which is immaculately maintained, can be visited. Slightly to the north, along the same street and in the midst of vineyards, is the squat Château Corton-Grancey. The Louis Latour estate (visits by appointment only) vinifies and ripens its wines in the château, which dates from 1834.

The local church.

Château Corton-André.

TOURIST TIPS
You get a beautiful view of Aloxe-Corton and its surroundings by driving towards Pernand-Vergelesses and then taking the first exit up the Corton hill.

Michel Voarick The wines made here are very traditionally vinified and are deliberately matured exclusively in wooden casks which have already been used. The quality of the whole range is very high; its six grands crus include Corton Clos du Roi, Romanée-St. Vivant and Corton-Charlemagne. All the red wines need to mature for years in the bottle.
Also Recommended Maurice Chapuis, Max Quenot Fils et Meuneveaux.

RELATED TO WINE
On the small village square there is a *caveau*, where the products of a number of winegrowers can be tasted.

The village was built beside a hill.

Restaurant Le Charlemagne
© 80.21.51.45
This establishment is situated at the foot of the village and specializes in regional dishes, such as *escargots, jambon persillé, caille vigneronne, boeuf bourguignon, coq au vin.* The quality is good and the two least expensive menus are certainly good value for money.

Pernand-Vergelesses

The rather insignificant Pernand-Vergelesses lies on the west side of the Corton hill, hidden in a valley. The name Pernand is derived from 'lost spring' and Vergelesses indicates the premier cru Les Vergelesses. The village was built beside a hill: the street leading into Pernand-Vergelesses winds upwards. At the first sharp turn is an old watering spot; near its wall tap a grape motif can be seen. The chapel of Notre-Dame de Bonne Espérance stands on the hill directly behind the village centre. It was built in 1854, in gratitude for the reconversion of a prominent woman to Catholicism. The view from the chapel on the hill is very fine indeed.

Recommended Producers

Domaine Bonneau du Martray One of the largest and most respected local properties, with land in the grands crus of Corton-Charlemagne and Corton.

Domaine P. Dubrueil-Fontaine Père & Fils Bernard Dubrueil sees his red Île des Vergelesses as 'a young girl, clothed in lace' and his three red Cortons as 'married women in their full glory'. Other fine wines from this large estate are Corton-Charlemagne and white Pernand-Vergelesses Clos Berthet.

Domaine Laleure-Piot White wines with a lot of fruit and of high quality, including Pernand-Vergelesses premier

Pernand-Vergelesses's most famous inhabitant was Jacques Copeau. After having made a name for himself in Paris as a theatrical innovator (in the Vieux-Colombier, which he founded), he settled in Pernand where, with young actors, he formed a new theatre group. It was called Les Copiaux, based on an idea from the local postman. The performances were announced by trumpet flourishes and often took place on squares and in parks. Copeau (1879-1949) lies buried in Pernand-Vergelesses. Although the village produces considerably more red than white wine, the white is generally more appreciated (it is the only one that has the name of the municipalty on it and it is also reasonably priced). In their youth red Pernand-Vergelesses tend to taste rather stiff and therefore benefit from ripening in the bottle.

Water from the tap, grapes on the stone.

Detail of the chapel.

Tourist Tips

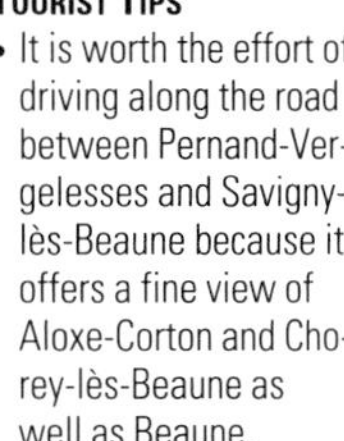

- It is worth the effort of driving along the road between Pernand-Vergelesses and Savigny-lès-Beaune because it offers a fine view of Aloxe-Corton and Chorey-lès-Beaune as well as Beaune.

- The village festival usually takes place on the first Sunday of August, near the chapel of Notre-Dame de Bonne Espérance.

cru and Corton-Charlemagne. Of the red wines, the Les Vergelesses and Île des Vergelesses have the most distinction.

Gabriel Muskovac Small wine estate.

Domaine Pavelot White Pernand-Vergelesses and Corton-Charlemagne are the best wines here, followed closely by the red premiers crus from the village itself.

Domaine Rapet Père & Fils Well-known, relatively large property. Among the most attractive wines are the white Pernand-Vergelesses Sous la Vierge, Corton-Charlemagne and the red Pernand-Vergelesses premier cru.

Also Recommended Denis Père & Fils.

In the park of Chandon de Briailles.

Savigny-les-Beaune

The history of Savigny goes back to the Gallic-Romanic period when a Roman road used to run through the municipality. Nowadays the village is a modern commuter suburb situated near Beaune. The old centre has quite a lot of atmosphere. The church, whose Romanesque, 12th-century clock tower has an octogonal spire, is situated in the middle of winding, narrow streets. Within, one of its art treasures is a 15th-century fresco with angels and saints. It is a few minutes' walk from the church to the castle, which is situated in the middle of a park on the south side of the village. The imposing building, which is flanked by round towers, nowadays functions as a museum. Apart from a few hundred motorcycles, the collection also

The local castle is also a museum.

Hotels

Lud'Hotel
✆ 80.21.53.24
Peacefully situated on the north side of the village. The hotel has existed since 1991 and has rather compact, modern rooms (a mere FF 300). Those in the more recent wing are more spacious and more expensive. Its restaurant (regional cuisine) is situated next to the tiny swimming pool. Directly behind the hotel you can begin a walk through woods and vineyards.

l'Ouvrée
✆ 80.21.51.52
About 20 rooms with reasonable comfort (about FF 250). Those at the rear are preferable: the hotel is situated next to the main road to Bouilland. The cooking is sound and the four-

Recommended Producers

Simon Bize & Fils Stylish, tasty and firm wines.

Bonnot-Lamblot Works traditionally.

Capron-Manieux Also white Savigny.

Domaine de Chandon de Briailles Rather large family estate whose wines are of immaculate quality. The estate not only has land in Savigny, but also in Pernand-Vergelesses and Aloxe-Corton. The best wines include Corton-Bressandes, Corton Clos de Roi and the very rare white Corton.

Maison Doudet-Naudin Good wine merchant.

Maurice Ecard & Fils Reliable.

Domaine Chandon de Briailles.

houses racing cars and aeroplanes (including a Mirage III). Visitors enter by way of an annexe, the so-called Petit Château, which dates from 1683 and was built in the form of an arch. If you drive in the direction of Beaune from the castle, you will see, in a side street to the right, the Manoir de Nicolay, a large mansion in Louis XIV style. Behind it is a marvellous garden laid out in the French style. The whole makes up part of the wine estate of Chandon de Briailles. Savigny-lès-Beaune has two sorts of vineyards. Those on the north side have a lot of lime in the soil and yield rather sturdy red wines (such as the premiers crus Aux Guettes Les Lavières, Aux Serpentières and Les Vergelesses). The soil on the south side contains more pebbles and gives more elegant wines (from, among others, La Dominode, Les Jarrons and Les Marconnets).

Wine aphorism above a doorway.

course menu is under FF 100. Behind L'Ouvrée – which has a small park – a wine hill rises up.

RESTAURANT
La Cuverie
✆ 80.21.50.03
Simple, restaurant situated on a street corner on the west side of the castle garden. Strict regional dishes (such as *fricassé d'écrevisses*); menus start at a mere FF 100.

TOURIST TIP
In the rue Chanoine Donin and the rue Guy de Vaulchier, among others, the façades have all sorts of wine aphorisms on them.

Domaine Antonin Guyon With about 50 hectares of wine land, this is the largest private estate of the Côte d'Or. The red, as well as the white wines, are characterized by a pure, lively taste with subtlety and an attractive wood/vanilla aroma.
Parigot & Richard Producer of Crémant de Bourgogne.
Pavelot-Glantenay Vital wines.
Domaine du Prieuré The wines here are tasted in an 18th-century cloister.
Henri de Villamont Swiss wine merchant.
Also Recommended Lucien Camus-Bruchon, Girard-Vollot & Fils, Pierre Guillemot.

Chorey-les-Beaune

The terrain of Chorey-lès-Beaune, a village just north of Beaune on the east side of the *route nationale*, is almost flat. That this is no handicap to making good wine is proven by the local estates because the best wines from the district have a rather sturdy structure and a soft fruitiness. This is the reason that they are increasingly sold under the name of the village itself; formerly most of them disappeared anonymously in Côte de Beaune-Villages.

The only interesting local building is the Château de Chorey. Its main building dates from the 17th century, while the towers that flank it are from the 13th century. Around the castle a moat and a park. Wine has been made here for centuries. Thus on beams in the *cuverie* a few striking harvest dates are carved. In 1893, for example, grape plucking had begun by August 28. Near Chorey Gallic-Roman finds have been made.

Château de Chorey.

Hotel

Château de Chorey
© 80.22.06.05
The castle has over eight large, comfortable rooms which are rented according to the chambre d'hôtes system. Prices start at about FF 600.

Restaurants

Le Bareuzai
© 80.22.02.90
Inside there is more atmosphere than the outside would lead you to expect. Regional dishes and more cosmopolitan ones, usually prepared with care. Menus start at FF 135 (plus inexpensive lunch menus through the week).

l'Ermitage-Corton
© 80.22.05.28
This is the *Maxim's* of the Côte d'Or, with a palace-like, lush interior. The cooking is excellent, inventive and ample. A large wine list. Menus start at about FF 300 (not on holidays). Through the week there is a lunch menu which costs about FF 180. It is also a luxurious hotel.

Recommended Producers

Arnoux Père & Fils Large property that makes sturdy, correct wines.

Château de Chorey/Jacques Germain The wines made here have a lot of allure, a tender taste and sufficient tannin. They come from Chorey itself as well as from Beaune and Pernand-Vergelesses (white).

Domaine Maillard Père & Fils Chorey-lès-Beaune, Beaune Grèves, Corton Renardes and other red wines.

Tollot-Beaut & Fils Civilized, harmonious red and white wines. Among the most captivating are Chorey-lès-Beaune, Aloxe-Corton, Beaune Clos du Roi and Corton-Bressandes.

Carriage in front of the Hôtel-Dieu.

Beaune

Beaune is situated near the intersection of two *autoroutes* and is therefore a favourite spot to spend the night – it has more than 35 hotels. The attractiveness of the city itself also draws visitors. The old centre is well preserved and unusually rich in atmosphere. Beaune was probably founded in AD 52 by Julius Caesar. At the beginning of the 13th century it received its town franchise because the Burgundian dukes often stayed here with great pleasure. A low point in Beaune's history was the fire of 1401, which destroyed three-quarters of all the houses. A few decades later the most famous building of the city was erected, the Hôtel-Dieu. It was commissioned by Nicolas de Rolin, who was a chancellor under Philip the Good. His wife, Guigone de Salins, decided to build a home for the sick and poor. It must have been quite an experience for the patients, because

Hotels

Belle Epoque
15 faubourg Bretonnière
✆ 80.24.66.15
Distinguished rooms and apartments. About FF 450.

Bellevue
5 route de Seurre
✆ 80.24.05.10
Simple, comfortable rooms (FF 150 to 175). Restaurant.

Hostellerie de Bretonnière
43 faubourg Bretonnière
✆ 80.22.15.77
A good place to stay close to the centre. Private car park. Ask for a room at the rear. Prices about FF 165 to 350.

Central Hôtel
2 rue Victor-Millot
✆ 80.24.77.24
Close to the Hôtel-Dieu. Pleasant rooms (starting at FF 400). Very good regional cuisine. Menus start at FF 130).

Le Cep
27 rue Maufoux
✆ 80.22.35.48
Luxurious, stylish rooms around a courtyard (starting at FF 550). In the restaurant, classically prepared dishes are served. The least expensive menu (about FF 170) is worth recommending.

Recommended Producers

Albert Bichot (6 bis boulevard Jacques Copeau) Modern and efficiently operating merchant which exports with much success. Many subsidiary labels.

Bouchard Aîné & Fils (36 rue Sainte-Marguerite) Most of the wines of this merchant are of average quality.

Bouchard Père & Fils A large portion of the wines that this firm produces come from their own land because Bouchard Père & Fils has more than 82 hectares of vineyards.

J. Calvet & Cie (6 Boulevard Perpreuil) Visitors are guided through 15th-century wine cellars.

La Closerie
61 route de Pommard
✆ 80.22.15.07
Modern hotel with good rooms, a garden and a swimming pool. Prices start at FF 320.
Colvert Golf Hôtel
Levernois
✆ 80.24.78.20
Modern hotel with 24 light, comfortable rooms (FF 320 to 350), next to Beaune's golf course.
Le Parc
Levernois
✆ 80.24.63.00
Rather rustic rooms (starting at about FF 200) with varying bathroom facilities. Very peacefully situated, next to the *Hostellerie de Levernois*.
Beaune also has a large number of formula hotels from chains such as *Altéa, Climat de France* and *Novotel*. Most of them are situated near the entry to the *autoroute*.

Restaurants
Au Bon Acceuil
La Montagne
✆ 80.22.08.80
On a hill near Beaune. Simple and inexpensive restaurant which is very busy. Strict, regional cuisine.

The colourful roofs of the Hospices de Beaune.

their accommodation had the air of a palace rather than that of a hospital. The ward looks on to a magnificent courtyard, where you look up to see a wooden veranda and gallery, with a multicoloured roof of glazed roof-tiles above them. Nowadays the monument is mainly used as a museum. Statues of Nicolas Rolin and his wife are situated in a courtyard behind the Hôtel-Dieu. In the course of the centuries, various benefactors have left no less than 60 hectares of wine land to the Hôtel-Dieu. The wines from this land are sold annually to benefit the collective hospitals of Beaune, the Hospices de Beaune. This takes place on the third Sunday of November, forming the world's largest charity auction. The selling of wines is the highlight of Les Trois Glorieuses, the three days of celebra-

Portal of the Collégiale Notre-Dame.

Domaine Cauvard Père & Fils (18 rue de Savigny) Quality conscious wine estate.
Champy Père & Cie (5 rue du Grenier à Sel) Estate dating from 1750. Reliable.
Chanson Père & Fils (10 rue du Collège) The red wines here generally taste light and discrete and are not very expressive.
Joseph Drouhin (7 rue d'Enfer) In quality, Drouhin is among the élite of Burgundian wine merchants. The wines – in part from their own estate of almost 60 hectares – have an unreproachable quality, as well as a charming fruitiness, much style and fine nuances. The firm has a cellar – opened in 1981 – which can hold about

tion, at which time, in Beaune and other wine municipalities, there are tasting sessions, ceremonies and receptions, as well as dinners: Les Chevaliers du Tastevin in the Château de Vougeot

Beaune has many attractive shops.

(Saturday evening) and Paulée de Meursault (Monday afternoon, see Meaursault). From the Hôtel-Dieu it is only a few minutes' walk to the other places of interest in Beaune, including the Musée du Vin de Bourgogne and the Collégiale Notre-Dame, a large Romanesque-Burgundian church (marvellous wall tapestries). The place Monge which has a 14th-century clock tower (*beffroi*) and the 16th-century Hôtel de la Rochepot (Gothic façade and two courtyards in the Italian Renaissance style) are also places of interest. Walking in a northerly direction, the Hospice de la Charité is reached. This is a former orphanage (collection of pewter). Still further north is the city hall, which also boasts two museums, the

Auberge Saint-Vincent
place de la Hall
✆ 80.22.42.34
Rustic, rather sober ambiance and regional dishes of reasonable quality for reasonable prices. Menus start at about FF 135.

Le Bistro Bourguignon
8 rue Monge
✆ 80.22.23.24
Wine bar, often with around 15 Burgundies, available by the glass. Inexpensive daily menu.

Chez Joël D.
45 rue Maufoux
✆ 80.24.71.28
Speciality: oysters and other *fruits de mer*. Friendly prices.

La Ciboulette
69 rue Lorraine
✆ 80.24.70.72
A pleasant place where you can dine well on fresh ingredients, for about FF 100 (sometimes even less).

l'Ecusson
place Malmédy
✆ 80.24.03.82
Rather chic restaurant, locally one of the best. Many original dishes. Menus start at about FF 120.

3500 casks.

Les Caves des Hautes-Côtes (route de Pommard) Co-operative of about 220 farmers.

Louis Jadot (5 rue Samuel Legay) A big name in Burgundy. This firm – which has had American owners since 1985 – has a strict policy of quality, with the result that the Burgundies of Jadot can be trusted blindly. They have a lot of character, aside from style and power.

Jaffelin (2 rue du Paradis) Sister firm of Boisset (Nuits-Saint-Georges).

Louis Latour (18 rue des Tonneliers) A family firm of high standing, which has a large press house with cellars in Aloxe-

Le Gourmandin
8 place Carnot
✆ 80.24.07.88
Inexpensive, regional dishes. Burgundies available by the glass or carafe.

Jacques Lainé
10 boulevard Foch
✆ 80.24.76.10
The cooking here is talented and careful. Meals are served on the terrace when the weather is good. Menus start at about FF 160.

Le Jardin des Remparts
10 rue de l'Hôtel-Dieu
✆ 80.24.79.41
Very refined, contemporary creations. The weekday lunch menu is about FF 120. Ordinary menus start at about FF 170.

Hostellerie de Levernois
Levernois
✆ 80.24.73.58
Jean Crotet has built a luxurious hotel complex surrounded by a park and next to a golf course, ten minutes' drive from Beaune. The cuisine is of a high quality (fresh regional ingredients). The weekday lunch menu is about FF 200, ordinary menus start at about FF 380.

Wine can be bought everywhere.

Musée des Beaux-Arts and the Musée Marey, devoted to Etienne-Jules Marey, who developed the basic principles of film technique.
Under Beaune a network of cellars spreads out. The largest complex is that of Patriarche Père & Fils; this estate receives about 100,000 visitors annually. The (unguided) tour through the cellars finishes with a tasting session. Wine can be

The stately home of Chanson Père & Fils.

Corton. The best red wines are usually those from their own estate which is over 40 hectares. Château Corton Grancey is the best known red wine but the white wines are generally of a higher quality.
Lycée Agricole et Viticole (16 avenue Charles Jaffelin) This school sells wines from its own land. Exemplary quality.

Patriarche Père & Fils (5-7 rue du Collège) Large wine merchant which has a large turnover of relatively inexpensive brand-name wines from outside Burgundy. Burgundies of quality can be found in the collection, which are usually generous and sturdy in taste. The cellars are certainly worth a visit.

In the wine museum.

bought everywhere in Beaune; there are many wine stores. Beaune also functions as the wine capital of Burgundy. Numerous wine agencies have their headquarters here and there are dozens of wine taverns. Beaune is also one of the largest wine towns of the Côte d'Or. The majority of the wine produced here is red. The wines seldom have striking individual characteristics, but does not alter the fact that the best premiers crus from the best producers help to explain why, centuries ago, Erasmus sighed that he wished to live in France, 'not to lead armies, but to drink the wines of Beaune'.

Hostellerie de la Paix
47 faubourg Madeleine
✆ 80.22.33.33
Two restaurants, the *Rôtisserie* (menus at about FF 120) and *Le Bouchon* (FF 100 or less), as well as a small hotel with 10 rooms (starting at FF 310).

Relais de Saulx
6 rue Louis-Véry
✆ 80.22.01.35
Small, stylishly decorated and generally busy restaurant with reliable, rather conservative, cuisine. Menus start at about FF 125.

Tourist Tips

- Beaune has a golf-course of 8 holes. It is situated in Levernois, on the other side of the *autoroute*.
- In Meursanges, after Levernois, you can book a balloon trip at the Château de Laborde.
- During the season, a *son et lumière* show takes place in the courtyard of the Hôtel-Dieu. Information at the Office du Tourisme.
- On Saturday morning there's a market in the city centre.

Domaine des Pierres Blanches (22 rue Richard) White and red Côte de Beaune.
Also Recommended Domaine Besançenot-Mathouillet (19 rue de Chorey), Albert Morot (Château de la Creusotte), Domaine des Terregelesses (25 Rue Pierre Joigneaux).

Related to Wine

Across from the Hôtel-Dieu, Patriarche Père & Fils and the Parisian publisher Flammarion have set up a documentation centre, the Athenaeum de la Vigne et du Vin. Exhibitions are set up here, while the library has 100,000 books about wine, Burgundy and gastronomy.

RESTAURANT
Café du Pont
✆ 80.22.03.41
In the dining room behind the bar, nutritious dishes such as *coq à la lie de vin* and *estouffade de boeuf bourguignon* are served for FF 100 or less. The Pommards start at about FF 120.

A few of the winegrowers advertise their cellars.

The cellar of Comte Armand.

Pommard

The wine village of Pommard is situated directly south of Beaune. It is easily recognized by its flat church tower. On the hills behind and to the south of Pommard the grapevines grow almost to the skyline. Once, however, this was different. For example, one of the premiers crus is called Les Epenots, a name which came about because pine trees used to grow on the same spot.

A street by a narrow canal.

For centuries pommard has enjoyed a good reputation for wine. It was praised by Henry IV, Louis XV and Victor Hugo, while the 16th-century poet Ronsard wrote: '...that in such a small place such a great wine could be born'. A true Pommard is characterized by a lot of colour and a lot of power; such a wine has to

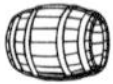

RECOMMENDED PRODUCERS
Comte Armand Pommard Clos des Epeneaux.
Domaine Billard-Gonnet Classic, initially introvert wines which need a long time in the bottle in order to develop.
Domaine Michel Gaunoux Concentrated Pommards (such as Rugiens and Grands Epenots).
Domaine Lejeune Perfect Pommards.
Domaine Mussy Traditional working estate with distinctive wines with longevity as well as power and variety.
Domaine Parent One of the largest local producers, with about 25 hectares of land, of which around one-third is in Pom-

ripen for a long time before its initial toughness changes into velvet. Unfortunately, not all Pommards satisfy this description: quite a few wines from this area are uninspiring, if not of average quality.

The driveway of Château de Pommard.

A busy departmental road runs straight through the village. To the side of this is found the surprisingly spacious church square, which is the heart of the village. In the church, which dates from the 18th century, woodcarvings can be admired. Some of the streets in Pommard are only four metres wide; they date from the days of the stagecoach. A narrow canal draws off water that streams down from the hills – and which, in the past, caused floods.

Tourist Tip
On the southeast side of the village, along the *route nationale*, a low, white, stone cross stands. At this spot there was once a ford in the Dheune river. The *croix de Pommard* is commemorated in the expression 'Tu n'es pas encore à la croix de Pommard', which means 'You are not at the end of your problems yet'.

On the church square.

mard. Reliable, expertly made wines, with various premiers crus in the leading role.
Château de Pommard This marvellously renovated wine estate attracts thousands of (paying) visitors annually. The wines from the 20-hectare, walled vineyard are sublime – and expensive.
Also Recommended Domaine de Madame Bernard de Courcel, Jean-Luc Joillot-Porcheray, Jean Michelot, Pothier-Rieusset.

Related to Wine

Across from the post office is Les Domaines de Pommard, a store where more than 20 producers sell their wines.

The church is Romanesque in origin.

Restaurants
le Cellier Volnaysien
✆ 80.21.61.04
This is the only restaurant in the village itself. It is situated near the church. One of the dining rooms is a vaulted cellar. On the menu only regional dishes (*oeufs en meurette, jambon persillé, coq à la lie*) are found. Various wines, also Volnays, are served by the glass. Menus start at a mere FF 100.

Volnay

Volnay, originally a Celtic village, is situated a few dozen metres above Pommard, against a wine slope. The northern entry is marked by a tasting centre and a giant bottle. Formerly, a castle, built by the first duke of Burgundy, stood at the end of the village. A 16th-century chapel is all that remains of it now. Most of the houses in the village itself date from the 17th and 18th centuries. The Romanesque church is actually 14th-century. Thanks to donations from the inhabitants, it has recently been completely restored.
Volnay's red wine has enjoyed great fame for centuries. In the 6th century it was drunk in Italy

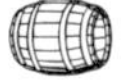

Recommended Producers
Domaine Marquis d'Angerville Producer of unusually handsome, remarkably fine and often velvety Volnays.
Domaine Yvon Clerget The Volnays of this small property are elegant and firm. On the contrary, the Pommard Rugiens tastes full and strong.
Bernard Glantenay Delicious Volnays with charm, suppleness and fruit.
Domaine Michel Lafarge One of the best local estates. The wines have colour, rounding and distinction – ordinary Volnay as well as the premiers crus.
Hubert de Montille A small estate with various great wines from Volnay as well

and in 1328 at the crowning of Philippe de Valois at Reims. After the conquest of Burgundy in 1477, Louis XI confiscated Volnay's entire harvest. Louis XIV and XV also drank this wine with pleasure.
The reason for all this is Volnay's character, because this red Burgundy excels due to its aroma and grace. In this village the finest red wines of the Côte de Beaune are made. The best Volnays come from premiers crus such as Caillerets,

Domaine de la Pousse d'Or.

The giant bottle just north of the village centre.

Champans, Clos de la Bousse d'Or, Clos des Chênes and Clos des Ducs. Wines from the premier cru Santenots bear the name Volnay, but come from land in Meursault.

Auberge des Vignes
✆ 80.22.24.48
Nice eating-house along the *route nationale*. In the rustic interior, very reasonably priced menus are served (two of them under FF 100). The menus contain regional, well-prepared dishes (such as *fricassé de volaille au Marc de Bourgogne*).

Tourist Tips

- By following a path upwards from behind the church (it says 'panorama' on a signpost), you will find a delightful viewing point. On clear days you can even see the Mont Blanc.
- Behind Volnay, in the direction of Meloisey, the remains of a Roman road and two dolmens can be found (along the D 17).

as Pommard. They are made traditionally and not filtered. Above all, the Volnay-Champans, Volnay-Taillepieds and Pommard-Rugiens deserve attention.
Domaine de la Pousse d'Or This estate, which was restructured in 1964, offers the very best of Volnay and works to the highest standards. Sublime, civilized, balanced Volnays (such as Clos de la Bousse d'Or) and delicious wines from Pommard and Santenay.
Joseph Voillot Average-sized winegrower with significantly more land in Pommard than in Volnay. His Volnays demand patience.
Also Recommended Bitouzet-Prieur.

Château de Monthelie.

Monthelie

The silhouette of this small wine municipality to the south of Volnay is characterised by two towers, both with multicoloured spires. The higher of the two towers is that of the 12th-century Romanesque church. Inside, there are many tombstones; one of them serves as an altar. The other tower is that of Château de Monthelie. It is older than the rest of the complex. By walking through Monthelie, you will discover a number of buildings from the 16th, 17th and 18th centuries. Almost all of them are inhabited by winegrowers because the area lives from wine and other types of plants or crops are not grown here. The wines of Monthelie are almost exclusively red and remind one of those from Volnay – although in a somewhat less fine and soft form. For this reason, their price is usually a bit friendlier.

Monthelie seen from tMeursault.

Tourist Tip

- It is useful to know that the village name is pronounced as 'Mont'lie'. In many books the name is spelt incorrectly, with an accent on the first 'e'.
- This village has known many owners, such as the monastery of Cluny. In 1730, it was bought by a pharmacist from Beaune!

Straight ahead for wine.

Recommended Producers

Denis Boussey Monthelie Champs Fulliots.
Xavier Bouzerand Expertly made wines.
Michel Deschamps Has two 18th century cellars.
Gérard Doreau Les Champs Fulliots.
Michel Dupont-Fahn Also Meursault.
Château de Monthelie The castle itself could do with a thorough cleaning up but the wine produced can withstand any criticism.
Potinet-Ampeau Classically worked wine estate.
Also Recommended Dom. Changarnier, Guy Dubuet.

Auxey-Duresses

View of Auxey-Duresses in early spring.

The *départementale* from Beaune to Autun winds through Auxey-Duresses. Auxey-le-Petit and Melin also make up part of the municipality. The most important place of interest in Auxey-Duresses is the church, whose clock tower has been declared a monument. Inside, you will find a triptych with depictions from the life of the Virgin, presumably created by Flemish hands. The weatherbeaten, grey chapel of Auxey-le-Petit is also nice. On the plateau of Mont Mélian, below Auxey-Duresses, are the remains of a prehistoric settlement. Due to its difficult name, sometimes rather reseved taste and modest production, red Auxey-Duresses is a wine that is, for a large part, sold as Côte de Beaune-Villages. The white wine is a bit friendlier but less than half as much is made. In this village itself this wine is normally available.

Recommended wine producer.

Restaurant
La Crémaillière
✆ 80.21.22.60

In a chic interior you can enjoy regional specialities and local wines. There is usually a menu under FF 100; the next price is almost twice as much. The quality of the dishes is good and usually a few inexpensive wines are offered that are not on the wine list. For parties and suchlike, there is cellar space available.

The church of Auxey-le-Petit.

Recommended Producers
Gérard Creusefond Strong red wines.
Jean-Pierre Diconne Les Duresses.
Domaine André et Bernard Labry This good estate is situated in the hamlet of Melin.
Henri Latour Modern equipment.
Leroy An almost legendary, small wine merchant firm which has made a speciality of thoroughly matured wines. In the cellars (situated next to the Watteau river, not far from the church) lie millions of bottles. Concessions concerning quality are not made here. Extremely high prices.
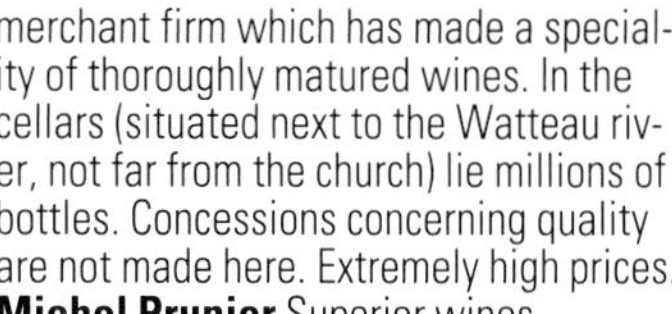
Michel Prunier Superior wines.
Also Recommended Roy Frères.

Restaurant
Hôtel-Restaurant Les Roches
© 80.21.21.63
The service in this rural hotel is friendly and the menus (starting at about FF 100) consist of regional dishes *(coq au vin, poulet de Bresse aux morilles et à la crème)*. A few simple hotel rooms with varying bathroom facilities.

Saint-Romain

A narrow, winding road leads from Auxey-Duresses (by way of Auxey-le-Petit) to the village of Saint-Romain. It consists of a high and low part, completely separated from each other. Thus, Saint-Romain-le-Haut is situated a few dozen metres above Saint-Romain-le-Bas. The elevated village area attracts quite a few visitors on Sunday afternoon, after the weekly family meal, because a local society has set out a good walking track around the remains of the former castle. The remains themself are not really impressive, but the view across the valley, in which Saint-Romain-le-Bas is situated, is often fine. In the higher village area there is also a 15th-century church with a sturdy tower in Romanesque style, a sloping nave and a sculptured pulpit from 1619. The caves, in which numerous archaeological finds have been made, prove that people lived near Saint-Roman as far back as prehistoric time. The community was a practically forgotten wine village until Roland Thévenin became mayor. He helped it gain a reputation by presenting Saint-

Saint-Romain-le-Haut (left) and le-Bas (foreground).

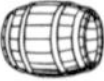

Recommended Producers
Domaine Henri et Gilles Buisson Average-sized wine estate with more than a dozen hectares, not only inSaint-Romain but also in six other areas of the Côte de Beaune. The white and red wines are of a good average quality.
Bernard Fèvre Small property, reliable red Saint-Romain.
Taupenot Père & Fils Locally, this is the fifth largest estate. Very decent red Saint-Romain and Auxey-Duresses. Soft, fresh white with the same titles of origin.
Domaine René Thévenin-Monthelie & Fils Delicious white and red wines with a lot of charm, such as the white and

Romain and its wines perfectly at the exchange in Dijon. This took place in 1962 with the theme of 'Mon Village'. For a long time this was used on labels, brochures and signposts. You will still see it on a few route signs. The red wines of Saint-Romain belong to the lighter type of Burgundy and often have a cherry-like fruit and agreeable suppleness. The white is not really full, but it certainly has its merits, thanks to a fresh taste with juiciness and sufficient fruit. In general, the quality of the white is somewhat higher than that of the red.

The 15th-century church.

Famous cooperage.

Tourist Tips

- In the town hall a small exhibition of the archaeological finds that have been excavated near Saint-Romain can be viewed.
- In the village there are two coopers, Claude Gillet and François Frères. The latter is very well-known and delivers vats to producers all over the world. The business is situated close to the Les Roches hotel-restaurant.

The lower part of the village.

red Saint-Romain, red Monthelie and red Beaune. The family owns about 16 hectares of wine land.

Hotels

Les Arts
✆ 80.21.20.28
Spartan rooms, creaking hall floors, loud water pipes: simple country hotel for guests who sleep soundly. Prices start at about FF 120. You can eat well and inexpensively in the restaurant (*boeuf bourguignon à l'ancienne*).

Les Charmes
✆ 80.21.63.53
Two styles of rooms: light and modern or classic. Both are tastefully and comfortably furnished. Friendly reception. Swimming pool. Prices start at about FF 400.

Les Magnolias
✆ 80.21.23.23
Extremely pleasant hotel in a renovated, 18th-century building opp. the Domaine Prieur. A dozen rooms (starting at FF 350).

Le Mont Mélian
✆ 80.21.64.90
In the centre. Twelve rather light, quite rustic rooms with a reasonably large bathroom. The owner offers visitors free bicycles and maps of the cycling routes. Prices about FF 250.

The marvellously restored city hall.

Meursault

Anyone visiting Meursault knows immediately that it's a wine village, because winegrowers' signs hang on numerous façades. White wine is in the majority here: Meursault produces ten times as much white as red. It is also the white wine that has given Meursault its international name. This wine has a fine, almost buttery taste, with the tones of ripe, sun-drenched fruits, nuts and toasted bread. A characteristic Meursault also contains sufficient acid to remain vital for decades. The best wines come from six premiers crus: Les Perrières, Les Genièvres, Les Poruzots, Les Charmes (the largest), La Goutte d'Or and Les Bouchères.
There are various opportunities annually to taste Meursaults. The most famous is the Paulée de Meursault, on the third Monday in November, at the close of Les Trois Glorieuses (see Beaune).

Recommended Producers

Raymond Ballot-Millot & Fils The average quality is high.
Château Génot-Boulanger Large wine estate.
Henri Germain Eminent wines.
Patrick Javillier Dynamic winegrower.
François Jobard Aristocratic Meursaults.
Château de Meursault At the castle grapes from over 40 hectares are processed.
Raymond Millot & Fils Attractive Meursaults.
Pitoiset-Urena Intense Meursaults.
Ropiteau Frères Wine merchant.

The event consists of an afternoon meal, usually of six courses, in the *cuverie* of Château de Meursault. The tables are laden with dozens of bottles. At the beginning of September a similar event is held, the Banée de Meursault. On the following day a large tasting session takes place, the Trinquée de Meursault.

Château de Meursault.

The Château de Meursault is the most important public building of the municipality. Above ground, as well as in the 12th- and 14th-century cellar complex, you can enjoy paintings with wine themes and taste the marvellous wines that the castle produces. Another castle is situated in the centre of the village. It has a fine multicoloured roof and nowadays functions as the town hall. It looks out over the 14th-century church of Saint-Nicolas, whose tower has a striking, Gothic spire.

One of the better hotels.

Restaurants
Hôtel du Centre
© 80.21.20.75
Affordable, regional dishes. The menus begin under FF 100. It also has a few hotel rooms.
Relais de la Diligence
© 80.21.21.32
Large business, a few kilometres from the village centre, on the other side of the *route nationale*. The interior is chic. Many menus. The second, most inexpensive one costs about FF 110 and offers very good value for money (*aiguillette de boeuf à la moutarde ancienne*).

Tourist Tips
The hamlet of l'Hôpital de Meursault has tasting rooms and touristy restaurants.

Domaine Rougeot Talented white wines.
Philippe Thevenot Small production.
Also Recommended Robert Ampeau & Fils, Pierre Boillot, Hubert Bouzereau-Gruyère, A. Buisson-Battault, Jean-François Coche-Dury, Dom. des Comtes Lafon, Dom. Darnat, Bertrand Darviot, Gabriel Fournier, Maison Jean Germain, Dom. Albert Grivault, Dom. Joseph Matrot, Michelot-Buisson, Pierre Millot-Battault, Dom. René Monnier, Dom. Jean Monnier & Fils, Pierre Morey, Pierre Perrin-Ponsot, Dom. Jacques Prieur, Dom. Guy Roulot.

Restaurant
Le Montrachet
✆ 80.21.30.06
Regional dishes are cooked with flair, while the menu also offers modern, inventive dishes. Menus begin at about FF 150. The wine list contains a marvellous collection of white and red Burgundies. Aside from costly wines, there is often a terrific Aligoté. Le Montrachet also has about 30 rooms, usually furnished with old furniture.

Puligny-Montrachet

Without prior knowledge, no one would suspect that Puligny-Montrachet produces a few of the world's greatest and costliest white wines, because the village has no allure. It consists of boring streets which lead to two spacious squares. The only building of any importance is Château de Puligny-Montrachet. In 1986, it was bought,

Signposts near Le Montrachet.

in a rather neglected state, by the Domaine Laroche from Chablis. Since then the building has been radically restored. Visitors are welcome and wine can be tasted. It is worth the effort to visit the partially 13th-century church because it has a marvellous choir from the 15th century. The true greatness of Puligny-Montrachet is not found above ground but in the ground itself, because the village's soil is per-

Château de Puligny-Montrachet.

Recommended Producers

Louis Carillon & Fils This average-sized estate produces, among others, a number of vital, fine premiers crus from Puligny-Montrachet.

Chartron et Trébuchet A wine merchant with has stringent quality control.

Domaine Henri Clerc & Fils Large property with land in no less than three grands crus. The wines are unusually reliable.

Domaine Leflaive The white wines produced here are distinguished by their rich nuances. Included in the brilliant collection are Bâtard-Montrachet, Chevalier-Montrachet, Bienvenues-Bâtard-Montra-

Hotel-restaurant.

fectly suited to the chardonnay grape. In the most famous vineyard, Le Montrachet, the soil contains a lot of lime and various other minerals. The direction of the sun's rays and the drainage are very favourable. Together, these natural factors result in an almost decadent white wine, aromatic, tasty and full of exciting nuances. Alexandre Dumas (1802-1870) was of the opinion that Le Montrachet should be drunk 'on your knees and with bared head', while someone else compared the bouquet to singing in a Gothic cathedral.

Next to the field of Le Montrachet (of which almost half belongs to the municipality of Chassagne-Montrachet), three other grands crus are situated: Bâtard-Montrachet, Bienvenues-Bâtard-Montrachet and Chevalier-Montrachet. Quite beautiful white wines are produced here as well. The premiers crus and even the white municipal wines of Puligny-Montrachet can also be delicious.

Tourist Tip
Against a slope on the border between Puligny-Montrachet and Meursault, lies the hamlet of Blagny, whose vineyards give a nice, if somewhat stiff, wine. From Blagny there is a fine view of Puligny and Meursault. Once there were quarries near Blagny. The stone for the 50-step staircase of the Hôtel-Dieu in Beaune came from these quarries in 1441.

Gateway to Le Montrachet.

chet and, since 1992, Montrachet. What's more, the range includes marvellous premiers crus, an excellent municipal wine and an attractive red Blagny.

Olivier Leflaive Frères Small, successful wine merchant who has made a speciality of high-quality white Burgundies.

Vve Henri Moroni Modest estate with, among others, a excellent Bâtard-Montrachet.

Paul Pernot & Fils A rising star that makes a few impressive white wines, including Puligny-Montrachet Folatières and Pucelles and a Bâtard-Montrachet.

Domaine Etienne Sauzet Sublime white wines with depth and distinction.

The village has a fine church tower.

Saint-Aubin

Puligny-Montrachet and Chassagne-Montrachet are separated by the N 6. If this is followed for a few kilometres in a northwesterly direction, *Gamay* first comes into sight and then, directly afterwards, the wine district of Saint-Aubin, to which this hamlet belongs. It is worth the effort of driving into Gamay, because the castle of the *seigneur* Du May, who, according to tradition, brought back an unknown grape variety from the crusades, is situated in the village. This variety received the name gamay. The weatherbeaten, grey Château de Gamay cannot be visited but you can drive around it. The same road – a former Roman *via* – leads, by way of the vineyards, to nearby Saint-Aubin. The streets here are narrow, without pavements and, as a rule, sloping. The central feature of the village is the church, dating from the 10th century. The striking, grey-stone clock tower dates from the 11th and 12th centuries. *Saint-Aubin* also has a castle. It was built in 1850 on the foundations of a medieval fortification. It is the property of a winegrower, Denis Blondeau-Danne, who uses the consistently cool cellars for maturing his better wines. Because Saint-Aubin is separated from Chassagne-Mon-

Restaurant
Auberge de la Chatenière
✆ 80.21.34.87
This is a very simple eating-house in the hamlet of Gamay. You can have sandwiches or complete menus costing well below FF 100. Locally, the business is also called 'Chez Mireille'.

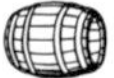

Recommended Producers

Jean-Claude Bachelet In Gamay. He is stronger in white than in red wines, with Bienvenues-Bâtard-Montrachet as the showpiece.

Domaine Blondeau-Danne An estate that works traditionally.

Raoul Clerget Absolutely serious and reliable wine merchant who, apart from purchasing wines, offer wines from their own estate, such as the distinctive white Saint-Aubin Le Charmois (from the Domaine du Pimont, a vineyard high on the border between Saint-Aubin and Chassagne-Montrachet) and white and red Saint-Aubin Les Frionnes.

trachet by a range of hills, the climate there is drier, cooler and gets snow in the winter. In the years 1970 and 1980, a number of winegrowers replanted fallow vineyards. In Saint-Aubin more premiers crus are produced than municipal wines. The white wines often have an agreeable aroma of hazelnut and a soft freshness and they form an affordable alternative to more expensive wines from other districts. The red tastes rather firm, with a touch of earthiness.

The castle of Gamay.

Sign in Saint-Aubin.

Roux Père & Fils This is one of the largest private producers and also a vintner. The best estate wines are the Saint-Aubin La Pucelle and La Chatenière.
Also Recommended Marc Colin, Hubert Lamy, Larue.

Related to Wine

In 1395, the gamay was banned in the Côte d'Or by Philip the Bold, because this grape gave such meagre wines. Nowadays the same grape is the basis for all red Beaujolais, most of the red Mâcon and is one of the two grapes used for Bourgogne Passetoutgrains.

Hôtel Sainte-Marie
Nolay
✆ 80.21.73.19
In a rustic ambiance, you can eat rural dishes, including *jambon persillé* and *oeufs en meurette*. Friendly service. It is also a hotel, but some of the very simple rooms are situated on a busy street.

Hautes-Cotes de Beaune

West of Corgoloin, Hautes-Côtes de Nuits borders on the district of Hautes-Côtes de Beaune. The latter consists of a northern and southern part, separated by the *autoroute*. The southern part is the nicest and the following route has been set there. It begins in Saint-Aubin. The first stop is *Nolay*, with a charming centre: half-timbered houses, a church with a striking stone spire and a 14th-century market hall (-place Monge). Nearby is the statue of Lazare Carnot, 'the organizer of the conquest' during the French Revolution. From Nolay it goes to *La Rochepot*, a village dominated by a powerful, restored castle in the style of the late Middle Ages. It has six pepper pot towers, a Chinese room and a Gothic chapel. Near the entrance, a local farmer usually lets his wines be tasted. In the village itself is an ancient, 12th-century church.
The church of *Baubigny*, the next village, also dates from the same century. The route now runs to

Baubigny, with its 12th-century church.

In the rosé village of Orches.

Restaurants
Chez Denise
Evelle
✆ 80.21.70.38
In the hamlet of Evelle, not far from Orches, Denise Lagelée cooks tasty regional dishes in an unpretentious, cosy ambiance. All this can be had for less than FF 100 a menu.

Recommended Producers
Domaine François Charles & Fils
(Nantoux) In the centre of the village the Charles family makes good wines, not only from the Hautes-Côtes, but also a Beaune Les Epenottes and a Volnay Les Fremiets.
Guillemard Dupont & ses Fils (Meloisey) Here you will find red as well as white wines of better than average quality. Some of the whites are bottled *sur lie*. Part of the production is sold under the name of André Guillemard-Pothier. Red and white Bourgogne Hautes-Côtes de Beaune, Beaune Grèves, Beaune Clos des Coucherias and many other premiers

Tasting room near Château de Rochepot.

Orches, below an imposing cliff. Above the village is a small well with a few Gallic-Roman gravestones nearby. Not far beyond Orches – known for its light, cheerful rosé – there is a spectacular panorama across Saint-Romain, with the Côte d'Or behind it. Now take the narrow road to the winegrowers' village of *Meloisey*, with its monumental church tower. Follow the road to *Mavilly-Mandelot* and *Mandelot* (16th-century castle). Finally, head in the direction of Pommard, with a stop in *Nantoux*, known for its good wines and its 15th-century church. In Hautes-Côtes de Beaune the grapes ripen quicker than in Hautes-Côtes de Nuits, which makes the wines somewhat sturdier. Almost twice as much wine is produced here, with the emphasis slightly more on red.

The covered market of Nolay.

Tourist Tips

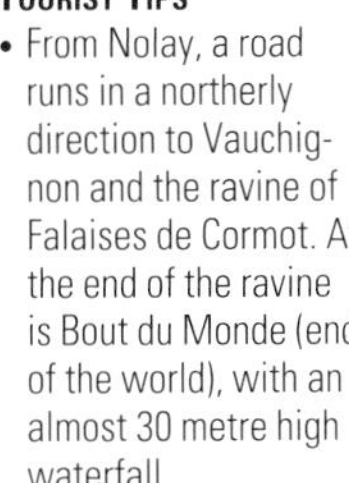

- From Nolay, a road runs in a northerly direction to Vauchignon and the ravine of Falaises de Cormot. At the end of the ravine is Bout du Monde (end of the world), with an almost 30 metre high waterfall.
- In various villages of Hautes-Côtes de Beaune and in Saint-Romain there are signposts for walks.
- Andrée Bouchard has written a book about Nantoux. It is called *L'eau et le vin.*

crus from Beaune are specialities.

Domaine Fouquerand Père & Fils (La Rochepot) At the foot of the local castle successful red and white Hautes-Côtes de Beaune may be tasted, as well as Volnays and a Santenay-Comme.

Domaine Lucien Jacob (Echevronne) An extremely hard-working, large wine estate offering, among others, red Hautes-Côtes de Beaune, Savigny-lès-Beaune and a white Savigny-Vergelesses.

Also Recommended Domaine Joliot (Nantoux), Mazilly Père & Fils (Meloisey), Domaine des Vignes des Demoiselles (Nolay), Parigot Père & Fils.

Chassagne-Montrachet

The peace of present-day Chassagne-Montrachet doesn't lead one to suspect that it has had a bloody history. In the 15th century, John of Chalon, Prince of Orange, decided to oppose Louis XI. As a result, the king proclaimed that the prince must hang and that all his possessions should be burnt. After a series of skirmishes, John retreated to the castle of Chassagne but the situation there became impossible so the prince fled, abandoning the unprotected village. The attackers began to plunder and murder. As a result, ancient Chassagne and its castle went up in flames and the inhabitants received the nickname 'the crushed'. The spot on which the fortress once

Tourist Tips

- In Chassagne-Montrachet there are two castles, both rectangular in form and, from an architectural point of view, not particularly interesting. They are both the property of winegrowers. The buildings are called Château de Chassagne-Montrachet and Château de la Maltroye. The latter can be recognized by its colourful roof.
- Before Chassagne was known for its wines, the village lived mainly from quarries. For five centuries they have produced a pink stone

The city hall.

'The best white wines in the world...'

Recommended Producers

Domaine Guy Amiot-Bonfils Since the second half of the 1980s the wine quality here has greatly increased, with magnificent wines as the result. These wines are also sold under the name Domaine Pierre Amiot.

Blain-Gagnard Eminent white wines.

Jean-Noël Gagnard Generous white wines.

Bernard Moreau Reliable in every respect.

Bernard Morey Strong in white premiers crus.

Jean-Marc Morey Extremely quality-conscious, unusually trustworthy wine-

Statue in the abbey of Morgeot.

stood is the highest part of the village. Here and there you can still see an old well or a piece of wall from the vanished castle. The main buildings now are the houses of winegrowers. The streets in the higher part of the village are winding and narrow. In the lower part they become somewhat straighter and wider. Here the church, the smart-looking *hôtel de ville* (also a school) and the *caveau* can be found.

that, when polished, looks very much like the marble that comes from Comblanchien.

On the same day as neighbouring Puligny, Chassagne added the name of its most famous vineyard to its own. Thus, on November 27, 1879, Chassagne became Chassagne-Montrachet. Apart from part of the grand cru Le Montrachet, the municipality also owns part of Bâtard-Montrachet and the entire, 1.6 hectares of Criots-Bâtard-Montrachet. In contrast to Puligny, Chassagne produces more red than white wine but the white wines are of better quality.

Skilful ironwork near Bachelet-Ramonet.

grower. Delicious white premiers crus.
Marc Morey Very pure white Burgundies with an elegant firmness that is well supported by wood. The red Caillerets is also quite delicious.
Michel Niellon Sublime grands crus.
Paul Pillot Sumptuous white premiers crus.
Domaine Ramonet The foremost property in Chassagne: fantastic white wines of all qualities (from municipal wine to Montrachet) and exceptional reds such as Clos de la Boudriotte, Clos St. Jean.
Also Recommended Dom. Bachelet-Ramonet, Georges Déléger, Gagnard-Delagrange.

Santenay

Just like Chassagne-Montrachet, Santenay is made up of a higher and a lower village, although these are situated much further away from each other. Close to Santenay-le-Haut is the hamlet of Saint-Jean, which also belongs to the municipality. The church here, named after Saint-Jean-de-Narosse, is from the 13th century and, apart from a wooden entrance hall, it also has two charming statues from the 16th and 17th centuries. Directly behind Saint-Jean rise steep cliffs which surround the entire village on the west side.

Before it made wine, Santenay was known for its water, which has healing qualities and originates from two

The only casino in the Côte d'Or.

Santenay-le-Haut.

Restaurants

l'Ouillette
✆ 80.20.62.34
An established name in Santenay. People from the village and its surroundings come here to enjoy regional dishes such as fillet of perch in Aligoté sauce, *coq au vin* and *entrecôte grillée* in a rustic ambiance. Menus start at FF 75.

Le Terroir
✆ 80.20.63.47
Situated next to *l'Ouillette*. Pleasant interior, good service and dishes that are somewhat less conventional than those of its neighbour. Thus there is always a fresh fish of the day, sometimes they serve pasta and you can

Recommended Producers

Adrien Belland Average-sized estate.

Domaine Josep Belland With more than 20 hectares, this is one of the most important local producers. The red wines (such as Santenay Clos du Beauregard) are often supple and juicy and the white Criots-Bâtard-Montrachet is excellent.

Domaine Lequin-Roussot The red wines of this rather large estate have often been crowned.

Prosper Maufoux Expert wine merchant, who generally has somewhat better quality white wines than red wines.

Jean Moreau/Domaine de la Buissière One of the best producers of

springs. Amoung other ailments, it helps against rheumatism. At one time the village was even called Santenay-les-Bains. Because it has the status of a health resort, French law allows it to have a casino, the only one in the Côte d'Or.

In the lower and larger part of the village, you can visit two interesting castles. Château Philippe le Hardi derives its name from the first duke of Burgundy (Philip the Bold) and has a massive, 14th-century castle tower. A wine museum is situated in the building. Wine is also made in the castle, in an ultra-modern *cuverie.*

A few dozen metres from the large village square is the Château du Passe-Temps. Its cellars are ten metres deep and are the largest of the Côte d'Or.

Santenay produces mainly red wines that are rather modest in nature; the best usually come from premiers crus 'east of the clock tower', such as Beauregard, Clos de Tavannes, La Comme and Les Gravières.

The church of Saint-Jean-de-Narosse.

order a 'surprise' menu. Menu prices start at about FF 75 (weekday lunch).

On the village square.

Santenay.

Mestre Père & Fils Large wine estate with distinctive red wines from various premiers crus in Santenay, plus wines from other districts.

Château Philippe-le-Hardi Most of the wines come from Mercurey and taste correct.

Domaine Prieur-Brunet Juicy, supple red wines with firmness and fine white premiers crus from Meursault. The cellars are also worth a visit.

Also Recommended Château de la Charrière, Michel Clair, Jessiaume Père & Fils.

Tourist Tip
From Dezize-lès-Maranges a road runs up to Mont de Sène (52 m). On its rather flat top there are three crosses. The view over Santenay is magnificent.

The Château de Mercey is situated near Cheilly.

Maranges

Just outside the department of Côte d'Or, but still belonging to the wine district of the same name, are three villages that form the *appellation* Maranges, which was created in 1989. They are, from north to south, Dezize-lès-Maranges, Sampigny-lès-Maranges and Cheilly-lès-Maranges. Winegrowing began in Dezize, where a Benedictine monastery was situated, but Cheilly has more wine land than the other two villages put together.

The church of Cheilly.

Dezize-lès-Maranges is reached by way of Santenay or via a beautiful road from Santenay-le-Haut. The village was built around an intersection of sloping streets. Close by is the grey-brown Romanesque church, dating from the 11th and 12th centuries. From Dezize the road winds down-

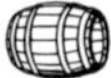

Recommended Producers

Domaine B. Bachelet & ses Fils (Dezize) Large estate that produces almost 20 different wines, from the Côte de Beaune as well as the Côte de Nuits. The reds are generally of good quality.

Domaine Gérard Berger-Rive (Cheilly) This rather large wine estate, which is situated in Mercey, produces a surprisingly good Aligoté. Another successful creation is the Crémant.

Domaine Fernand Chevrot (Cheilly) Situated in a large farm above the village. Attractive red wines, including Cheilly-lès-Maranges and Santenay Clos Rousseau. Fine 18th-century cellar.

wards to Sampigny-lès-Maranges, situated in a small, wooded valley that is fringed by cliffs. The village is ancient and picturesque; the church, built on raised ground, has a wooden tower. Cheilly-lès-Maranges stretches out across low hills and is surrounded by vineyards as well as lush pasture. The hamlet of Mercey, a few kilometres away, belongs to this municipality. The Château de Mercey, which is the centre of an important wine estate, was built four centuries ago. The wines of Maranges – mainly red – are rather light and fresh. They can taste very pleasant and are generally reasonably priced.

Dezize-lès-Maranges is built on a hill.

Crossroad in the middle of this little district.

Yvon et Chantal Contat-Grangé (Dezize) Modernly equipped business which was founded in 1980. Fine red and white Maranges.

René Martin (Cheilly) Although situated in Cheilly, Martin makes a nice-tasting red wine from Sampigny.

Domaine du Château de Mercey (Cheilly) A respected estate with vital, pure white wines (Aligoté, Hautes-Côtes de Beaune, Mercurey) and soft, civilized reds (Haute-Côtes de Beaune, Mercurey, Santenay).

Also Recommended La Cave de Cheilly, Maurice Charleux.

Chalonnais

The wine district of Chalonnais – or Côte Chalonnaise – is a direct continuation of the district of Côte d'Or, yet the landscape is different. Wine grapes alternate here with other types of plants and there are also many pastures and forests. The landscape is usually hilly and the grapevines are planted along slopes as well as on plateaus and in valleys.

The wines from Chalonnais are much less famous than those of the Côte d'Or. This is because in the past, in this northern district, they were usually sold by merchants – and only seldom under their own name. Nowadays Chalonnais actually has six *appellations* of its own. Five of these are connected to municipalities or groups of municipalities. In the north of this rather narrow, rectangular district, the rather boring city of Chagny is situated, with the hamlet of Bouzeron slightly to the south. Its Bourgogne Aligoté is so good that it may be sold under the name Bouzeron. The other municipal titles of origin are, from north to south, Rully, Mercurey (by far the largest), Givry and Montagny. The city of Chalon-sur-Saône does not make up part of the actual wine district, although *La Maison des Vins de la Côte Chalonnaise* is situated here, where wines from the whole district can be tasted and sold. Chalonnais also has a regional title: Bourgogne Côte Chalonnaise. This is valid for red and white Burgundies from 44 municipalities between and around the villages that belong to the municipal titles of origin. Bourgogne Côte Chalonnaise has not existed long: the first harvest to be sold in this way was that of 1989.

The hamlet of Palotte in northern Chalonnais.

Chalonnais also produces a rather large amount of Crémant de Bourgogne. This sparkling wine generally comes from Rully, where a number of businesses specialize in this type of wine.

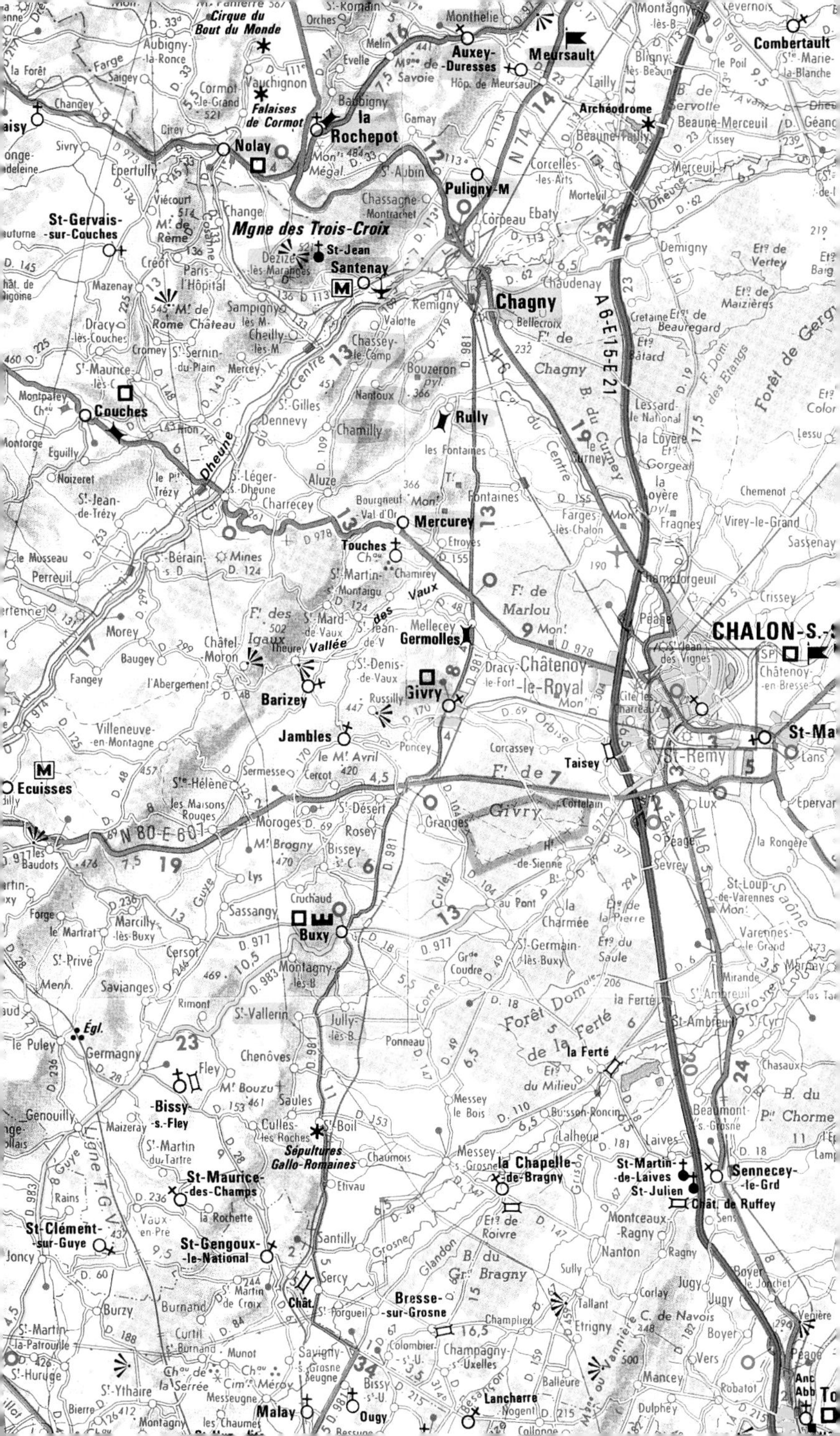

Cirque du Bout du Monde
Falaises de Cormot
Aubigny-la-Ronce
Vauchignon
Cormot-le-Grand
Nolay
la Rochepot
Mont Mégal
St-Romain
Orches
Melin
Evelle
Baubigny
Mgne de Savoie
Monthelie
Auxey-Duresses
Meursault
Hôp. de Meursault
Gamay
St-Aubin
Puligny-M
Chassagne-Montrachet
Corpeau
Ebaty
Chagny
Bellecroix
Chaudenay
Corcelles-les-Arts
Morteuil
Tailly
Bligny-lès-Beaune
Archéodrome
Beaune-Tailly
Beaune-Merceuil
Merceuil
Montagny-lès-B.
Levernois
Combertault
Ste-Marie-la-Blanche
Cissey
Demigny
Etg de Vertey
Etg de Maizières
Etg de Beauregard
Etg Bâtard
Forêt de Gergy
Lessard-le-National
la Loyère
Gorgeat
Fragnes
Virey-le-Grand
Chemenot
Sassenay
Champforgeuil
Crissey
CHALON-S.-
Châtenoy-en-Bresse
St-Jean des Vignes
St-Remy
Lans
Lux
Epervans
la Rongère
St-Loup-de-Varennes
Varennes-le-Grand
Marnay
Mirande
St-Ambreuil
St-Cyr
Chasaux
B. du Pt Chorme
Beaumont-s.-Grosne
Laives
St-Martin-de-Laives
St-Julien
Sennecey-le-Grd
Chât. de Ruffey
Montceaux-Ragny
Nanton
Ragny
Sully
Corlay
Jugy
Boyer
le Jonchet
Vers
Mancey
Robatot
Dulphey
Tallant
Etrigny
C. de Navois
Champlieu
Champagny-s.-Uxelles
Balleure
Lancharre
Nogent
Collonge
Bresse-sur-Grosne
Colombier-s.-U.
Bissy-s.-U.
Ougy
Malay
Savigny-s.-Grosne
Beugne
Sercy
Chât.
St-Porgeuil
Santilly
Etivau
Chaumois
Messey-s.-Grosne
la Chapelle-de-Bragny
Etg de Roivre
B. du Gr. Bragny
Lalheue
Buisson-Roncin
Messey le Bois
la Ferté
Etg du Milieu
Forêt Domle de la Ferté
St-Germain-lès-Buxy
Grde Coudre
Etg de la Pierre
Etg du Saule
la Charmée
au Pont
Hr de Sienne
Cortelain
Granges
Fr de Givry
Taisey
Corcassey
Dracy-le-Fort
Châtenoy-le-Royal
Cité les Charreaux
Fr de Marlou
Germolles
Mellecey
St-Jean-de-V.
St-Denis-de-Vaux
Russilly
Givry
Poncey
Jambles
le Mt Avril
Cercot
Sermesse
St-Désert
Rosey
Bissey-s.-C.
Moroges
Mt Brogny
Cruchaud
Buxy
Montagny-lès-B.
Jully-lès-B.
Ponneau
St-Vallerin
Chenôves
Saules
Mt Bouzu
Fley
Bissy-s.-Fley
Culles-les-Roches
St-Boil
Sépultures Gallo-Romaines
St-Maurice-des-Champs
la Rochette
St-Gengoux-le-National
St-Martin-de-Croix
Burnand
Curtil
Munot
Chau de la Serrée
Cimre Méroy
Messeugne
les Chaumes
Montagny
St-Ythaire
Bierre
St-Huruge
St-Martin-la-Patrouille
Burzy
Joncy
St-Clément-sur-Guye
Vaux-en-Pré
Rains
St-Martin-du-Tartre
Maizeray
Genouilly
Ligne T.G.V.
Germagny
le Puley
Égl.
Rimont
Savianges
St-Privé
Cersot
Marcilly-lès-Buxy
le Martrat
Forge
Sassangy
Lys
les Baudots
N 80-E 607
les Maisons Rouges
Ste-Hélène
Villeneuve-en-Montagne
Ecuisses
Fangey
l'Abergement
Baugey
Morey
Châtel-Moron
Barizey
Fr des Igaux
Theurey
Vallée des Vaux
St-Mard-de-Vaux
St-Martin-s.-Montaigu
Chamirey
Touches
Mercurey
Etroyes
Bourgneuf-Val-d'Or
Fontaines
les Fontaines
Rully
Farges-lès-Chalon
le Surney
B. du Curney
C. du Centre
Fr de Chagny
Bouzeron
Chassey-le-Camp
Nantoux
Chamilly
Aluze
Charrecey
St-Gilles
Dennevy
St-Léger-s.-Dheune
Dheune
Canal du Centre
St-Bérain-s.-D
Mines
Perreuil
le Musseau
St-Jean-de-Trézy
le Pt Trézy
Noizeret
Eguilly
Montorge
Couches
Montpaley
St-Maurice-lès-C.
Dracy-lès-Couches
Cromey
St-Sernin-du-Plain
Mercey
Cheilly-lès-M.
Sampigny-lès-M.
Mt de Rome Château
Mazenay
Créot
Paris-l'Hôpital
Dezize-lès-Maranges
St-Jean
Santenay
Remigny
Valotte
Mgne des Trois-Croix
Change
Mt de Rème
Viécourt
St-Gervais-sur-Couches
Epertully
Sivry
Cirey
Changey
la Forêt
Saigey
Farge
A 6-E 15-E 21
N 74
N 6

Hotels

Auberge du Camp Romain
Chassey-le-Camp
✆ 85.87.09.91
Very peacefully situated hotel with almost 45 rooms that offer a view across the valley. The interior is comfortable, without embellishments. In the restaurant the cuisine is rather traditional (starting at about FF 115 for a menu). Rooms start at approx. FF 300. Swimming pool.

Hostellerie du Château de Bellecroix
Chagny
✆ 85.87.13.86
Quite luxurious accommodation situated in a castle in a park. Rooms from FF 500. Excellent restaurant. Menus commence at around FF 200. Swimming pool.

One of the best hotels of this region.

Northern Chalonnais

The largest city in northern Chalonnais is *Chagny.* It has quite a lot of industry and only once a year is the emphasis on wine: during the wine exchange in the middle of August. In the centre of Chagny there are a few beautiful buildings from the 17th and 18th centuries, while, on the corner of the rue de la République and rue de la Boutière, there is a large medieval house. Behind the city hall is a garden with old wells and the remains of walls, while, in a chapel of the sober cistercian church, a replica of the grotto of Lourdes has been built. From Chagny a narrow road runs in a southwesterly direction to the hamlet of *Bouzeron.* This is the home of a superior Bourgogne Aligoté, which bears the

The church of Bouzeron.

Recommended Producers

Chanzy Frères Domaine de l'Hermitage (Bouzeron) This estate, which was founded in 1974, is among the best of Chalonnais. Above all, the white wines demand respect, such as those of the Clos de la Fortune.

Domaine du Château de Chamilly (Chamilly) Visitors are received in the 17th-century former kitchen.

Domaine de La P'tiote Cave (Chassey-le-Camp) Almost 15 different wines.

A. et P. de Villaine (Bouzeron) Aubert de Villaine is co-owner of the Domaine de la Romanée-Conti in Vosne-Romanée but with his wife Pamela also runs a very

municipality's name. Bouzeron consists of narrow, sloping streets and lies at the foot of an ancient, small, grey church. By taking a winding road across a hill crest, it is possible to reach the village of *Chassey-le-Camp* by way of *Nantoux*. It can be seen long before you reach it because it is situated in a valley. On the west side of the village the remains of a large Neolithic settlement (3200-2000 BC) were discovered in the 18th century. It is about 750 metres long. Since 1866 the settlement has been studied seriously, which has led to the excavation of thousands of objects. The spot can be reached on foot. The long walk doesn't offer many archaeological surprises but it does give a marvellous panorama across the broad surroundings. In *Chamilly*, just south of Chassey-le-Camp, there is a Romanesque church with stone statues from the Middle Ages; the local, constantly renovated castle is the property of a winegrower. In *Aluze*, once more to the south, the remains of a Gallic-Roman fortification have been discovered.

A peek at Bouzeron.

RESTAURANTS

Lameloise
Chagny
✆ 85.87.08.85
Three stars in the *Michelin Guide*. The cooking is fantastic and the wine list is sublime. Menus start at about FF 350. Also a hotel.

Relais Gaulois
Nantoux
✆ 85.87.33.00
Rustic inn on a hill crest. Regional dishes in menus under FF 100.

reputable property in Bouzeron. This produces exquisite wines, including the local Aligoté and an impressive white Burgundy, baptised Les Clous.

RELATED TO WINE

By taking the D 978 in a westerly direction slightly to the south of Aluze, you reach the Couchois, a group of wine municipalities that produce red and white Burgundy plus other generic wines. Included among these villages are Couches, Dracy-les-Couches and Saint-Maurice-les-Couches. The first two villages have impressive castles.

RESTAURANT
Hôtel du Commerce
✆ 85.87.20.09
It is situated on the place Sainte-Marie and has a rather chic and, at the same time, rustic dining room. There is always a choice of various menus with regional dishes (*truite à l'Aligoté, blanc de volaille vigneronne*) properly prepared. The most inexpensive menus cost less than FF 100. It is also a simple hotel.

RULLY

The rather strung-out village of Rully is situated just south of the city of Chagny. Arriving from there you soon see the first vineyards to the right of the road (D 981). They are planted along a wooded hill on which the Domaine de la Folie was built, a prominent wine property.
The oldest part of the village, where the church stands, is also on a hill. Most of the houses, however, are at the foot because, after the plague of 1347, the inhabitants

Château de Rully seen from its vineyard.

The church is situated in the elevated village.

RECOMMENDED PRODUCERS
Jean-Claude Brelière Passionate winegrower who, from his modest field makes a fresh, pure white Rully and a constantly improving red.
Michel Briday Delicious white wines.
André Delorme The elongated cellar complex of this dynamic business is situated behind the local church. Sparkling wines are mainly produced, for the business itself as well as for a number of winegrowers who do not have the knowledge and equipment for making Crémant de Bourgogne. The sparkling wines of Delorme itself are excellent. The same family runs the large Domaine de la

fled the old village and built a new community on lower ground. In this low village the streets are sometimes surprisingly broad. The village also has a number of stately mansions. The triangular place Sainte-Marie is an atmospheric square, with a park and a statue in the middle. There is also a nice view of the entire village.

The place Sainte-Marie.

The most important local building is Château de Rully. It is enthroned on a hill, splendidly preserved and flanked by three round towers. In addition, the château has a square tower, which dates from the 13th century; many of the other parts date from a later period. In front of the castle is a vineyard and, behind it, a park in the English style (it can be visited only during weekends).

Since the 1970s, winegrowing around Rully has experienced a revival. In general, the white wines – which are aromatic, fresh and fruity – have somewhat more depth than the red. Furthermore, much Crémant de Bourgogne is produced in Rully for local producers as well as by commission from farmers who have the necessary grapes but no equipment.

Tourist Tips

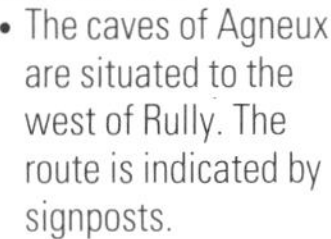

- The caves of Agneux are situated to the west of Rully. The route is indicated by signposts.
- Close to the church is a striking building with a small chapel near the gateway.

Renarde, which produces, among others, an attractive white Rully.

Domaine de la Folie Between Chagny and Rully stands a hill on which the Bouton family has created the 'estate of foolishness'. The wines – mainly white and red Rullys – are of top quality.

Henri et Paul Jacqueson Successful red wines from Rully and Mercurey; the white wine is not to be despised either.

Château de Rully The Antonin Rodet firm makes a fine white and red Rully which is marked by wood and vanilla.

Also Recommended Georges Duvernay/Domaine Saint-Michel, Dom. du Prieuré.

Mercurey

That Mercurey has, thanks to wine, known some periods of prosperity is indicated by the large winegrowers' houses to be seen in this village. Most of them were built in the 18th and 19th centuries. In and around Mercurey there are also a few castles. The *Maison du Mercurey* of the collective wine producers is located in Château de Garnerot, while Château de Chamirey (in the hamlet of the same name) is the property of the family that runs the Antonin Rodet wine tavern. A castle that has now disappeared was the medieval castle of Saint-Martin-sous-Montaigu; it was demolished by Henry IV and only a few ruins remain. Mercurey has well over 2000 inhabitants and consists mainly of one long street, which has striking copper lanterns. Near *Hostellerie du Val d'Or*, a side street runs upwards to Mercurey-le-Haut, where there is a Romanesque church from the 11th century. On the other side of Mercurey, also on a

Château de Chamirey of the Rodet estate.

Touches has an attractive church.

Restaurant
Hostellerie du Val d'Or
✆ 85.45.13.70
You can have a pleasant stay in this large inn. In the somewhat rustic dining room you can enjoy tasty dishes based on regional ingredients (*le feuilleté de grenouilles aux champignons*), while inventive creations are also offered in 'Ma cuisine du moment'. Impressive wine list. Menus start at FF 150 (weekday). The business also has over 13 quite spacious hotel rooms. It is essential to ask for a room at the rear because the traffic is noisy.

Recommended Producers

Domaine Bordeaux-Montrieux Supple, juicy, red Mercureys. The owner is the director of the Domaine Thénard in Givry.

Luc Brintet et Frédéric Charles Average-sized estate which produces pleasant-tasting Mercureys. The best age in new casks.

Michel Juillot This is one of the largest, local, private estates, with vaulted under an 18th-century building on the main street. The red wines taste rather firm and supple, while the white is also very successful.

Domaine de la Monette Sturdy type of

View across Mercurey.

hill, stands the attractive church of *Touches.* It was built between the 12th and 15th centuries and has a splendid clock tower situated in the middle of the nave. From Touches there is a lovely view of Mercurey. In Mercurey – the largest wine municipality of the Chalonnais – more than 90 per cent of the wine produced is red. This is usually robust and tasty, without being really refined but is furnished with fruit and tannin. Nowadays white Mercurey has more freshness and character than previously. It is striking that a lot of land is owned by firms and proprietors from the Côte d'Or, including Château Philippe-le-Hardi (Santenay), Faiveley (Nuits-Saint-Georges) and Bouchard Aîné (Beaune).

Tourist Tip
By driving from Mercurey to Givry, you pass Germolles, on the south side of which is an interesting castle whose oldest part dates from the 12th century. It was formerly owned by Philip the Bold and may be visited.

Many wine signposts.

red Mercurey.
Jean Maréchal They still work traditionally here.
Antonin Rodet Wine merchant
The quality of the Burgundies rose steadily in the 1980s. From its own land come the red and white Mercurey from Château de Chamirey (a hamlet near Mercurey).

Domaine de Suremain Aristocratic, complete Mercureys are made here.
Also Recommended Jeannin-Naltet Père & Fils, Dom. du Meix-Foulot/Yves et Paul de Launay, Yves Marceau/Domaine de la Croix Gault, Louis Menand Père & Fils, Dom. Fabien et Louis Saier, Emile Voarick (Saint-Martin-sous-Montaigu).

Hotel
Le Dracy
Dracy-le-Fort
✆ 85.87.81.81
This modern business is situated next to a large orthopaedic centre. The almost 40 rooms are comfortable (prices from about FF 300). In the *La Garenne* restaurant you can eat decently, starting at about FF 100. All in all, it is a good place to spend the night.

Restaurants
Auberge de la Billebaude
✆ 85.44.34.25
This rustic bistro, near the church, offers regional and other dishes at low prices. There is usually a fish menu and *fondue vigneronne*. On Saturday evenings, cabaret performances are given.

Givry

The winegrowers of this district will tell you that Henry IV's mistress Gabrielle d'Estrées liked to drink Mercurey but Henry himself preferred Givry. Of all the wine municipalities in the Chalonnais, Givry is the richest in history because its wine was already renowned in the 6th century and throughout the Middle Ages. Around 1780 the village functioned as the wine centre for the entire region and the enormous cellars of present-day Domaine Thénard bear testimony to this. Nowadays, there is little of this illustrious past to be seen. What's more, most of the winegrowers do not live in Givry itself but in neighbouring hamlets, such as Jambles, Poncey and Russilly. This does not mean, however, that Givry is not worth a visit. There are a few striking buildings. These include the Halle Ronde, along the main street, a round building with a spiral staircase (1830) inside. Not far away

Wine presentation at the post office.

The Halle Ronde.

Recommended Producers
René Bourgeon (Jambles) Active, small winegrower whose wines have received international awards.
Domaine Chofflet-Valdenaire (Russilly) The Chofflet family has made wine here since 1710. The red, as well as the white Givry, is very reliable.
Propriété Desvignes (Poncey) Average-sized estate, of which the white Givry is quite aromatic and the red Givry Clos du Vernoy has sufficient power and backbone to undergo bottle ageing.
Lumpp Frères Exemplary Givrys.
Domaine Ragot (Poncey) The white Givry here is generally more interesting than

The Porte de l'Horloge with its small church tower.

stands the town hall, completed in 1771 and built around a gateway, the Porte de l'Horloge, with its small clock tower. Once past the gateway you come to a large, rectangular square which is dominated on the north side by a post office that looks like a castle. Angels and grapes decorate the façade. From a distance you can see that the large, octagonal church (designed by Emile Gauthey, who also designed the town hall) is crowned by domes. There are also a few handsome fountains in Givry. The district of Givry mainly produces red wines. These have a firm silhouette and often a soft taste. The white wines taste fresh but at the same time firm, and are more or less aromatic.

Hôtel de la Halle
✆ 85.44.32.45
Typical country restaurant where the cooking is unpretentious but tasty (*rôtis, grillades, lapin aux deux moutardes, etc.*). The menus begin under FF 100. It is also a simple hotel.

Tourist Tip
In nearby Chalon-sur-Saône there is an 18-hole golf course.

the red. Small, vaulted tasting cellar.
Clos Salomon This estate, which dates back to the 14th century, produces only one wine, red Givry. It has a healthy colour, quite a bit of tannin and a pleasant dose of fruit.
Domaine Thénard The wines ferment and ripen here in 18th-century cellars. This prominent estate also has land in the Côte d'Or. In the high-quality range there are, among others, Le Montrachet, Grands Echézeaux, Corton Clos du Roi and various sorts of Givry.
Also Recommended André Gouot (Russilly), Gérard Mouton (Poncey), Dom. Gérard Parize Père & Fils (Poncey).

Chalon-sur-Saone

From Givry it is not far to Chalon-sur-Saône, the place from which the Chalonnais receives its name. With approximately 55,000 inhabitants, this city is the second largest in Burgundy, after Dijon and before Mâcon. Because of Chalon's location on the Saône, it has been a trade centre as far back as human memory. Its annual fairs were known throughout the whole of Europe. This is still the case for the Foire aux Sauvagines, a game market which takes place at the end of February. The suburbs of Chalon are completely uninteresting, but the old centre unquestionably has charm. It is situated, in the form of a fan, behind the river quay and has many half-timbered houses. Along the quay itself, on a small square, stands the statue of Chalon's most famous son; Nicéphore Nièpce (1765-1833). He made history by inventing photography. Near the statue is the Musée Nièpce, which is one of the most important photographic museums in the world. The history of photography is exhibited here in a fascinating way. In the collection are, among other things, the equipment of Nièpce (and his pupil Daguerre, who was able to shorten the exposure process) and the world's very first photos. Attention is also paid to modern equipment and contemporary photographs. In the museum there is also a design for a jet engine, another of Nièpce's inventions.

Jeu de boules near the Maison des Vins de la Côte Chalonnaise.

By walking into the centre from the above-mentioned statue, you soon arrive at the city hall square. Here stands the church of Saint-Pierre, a building mainly in Gothic style, which was completed in the 18th century. There are also some old statues. The Musée Denon, which was founded in 1819 in a former monastery, is on the same square. It has many finds from prehistoric times, including some from the excavation near Chassey-le-Camp, (see Northern Chalonnais) the Middle

Ages and later periods. Besides paintings, the collection also contains marvellous pieces of furniture, nautical instruments and Egyptian art. The founder of the museum, Dominique Denon (1747-1825), took part in Napoleon's Egyptian campaign and became a well-known egyptologist. Between the place de l'Hotel de Ville and the place Saint-Vincent, an attractive shopping street runs parallel to the quay. The square just mentioned is surrounded by half-timbered houses; also here is the 15th-century Maison aux trois Greniers with its balustrades. The church of Saint-Vincent has the allure of a cathedral but, because it was built and rebuilt between the 12th and 19th centuries, it displays various architectural styles and therefore lacks harmony as a whole. On one side is a cloister with three galleries. From the church it is not a long walk to the Promenade Sainte-Marie. The chalet-like *Maison des Vins de la Côte Chalonnaise* is situated here. This is a promotion centre for wines from the Chalonnais. Dozens of wines of every *appellation* can be bought here to drink at home. They are selected by a jury of experts. The wines can also be tasted and on the first floor there is a simple restaurant, *La Feuillette*, where, at low prices, regional and grill dishes are served. *Jeu de boules* is often played near the centre. From Chalon's centre, a bridge runs to the Ile Saint-Laurent. On the west side of this small island, next to an enormous lime tree, stands the Tour du Doyenné. It is hexagonal and dates from the 15th century. At certain times it can be climbed; there is a beautiful view of the city centre. The tower once stood next to the Saint-Vincent but, with the help of a rich American, it was moved, stone by stone, to its present location in 1926. Golf lovers will enjoy themselves in Chalon-sur-Saône, where on the east bank, in a bend of the river, the city has laid out a fine, 18-hole golf course.

The statue of Nièpce.

Hotels

Château Sassangy
Sassangy
✆ 85.96.12.40
In this 18th-century castle, which has been entirely renovated, six rooms are available, following the *chambre d'hôte* formula. Peace, stylish comfort and hospitality are the keywords here. Prices start at about FF 450. It is possible to order a dinner. Sassagny is situated a few kilometres west of Buxy.

Le Relais du Montagny
Buxy
✆ 85.92.19.90
This hotel was opened in 1990 and is near the local co-operative. Its 30 rooms are neat, not all spacious and functionally furnished. There is a swimming pool. The same owners as *Girardot.*

Montagny

That the wines of Montagny, the southernmost district of the Chalonnais, were formerly sold as Côte de Buxy is understandable because, apart from Montagny-lès-Buxy, the title of origin of Montagny consists of Buxy, Jully-lès-Buxy and Saint-Vallerin – of which Buxy is by far the largest district. The only wine co-operative of the district is also found here. The wines of Montagny are exclusively white and are characterized by a sturdy, juicy taste and a light, nut-like aroma. The ratio between price and quality is one of the strongest in Burgundy.

In the 12th century, the village of *Buxy* was fortified, of which two towers are the only reminder. Near the Tour Rouge, there is a large, charming wall painting which, in a playful way, sheds light on the wines from the district. The church has a striking tower and has been rebuilt various times.

The wine village of Montagny.

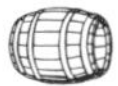

Recommended Producers

Pierre Bernollin (Jully-lès-Buxy) A good place for Montagny as well as Crémant de Bourgogne.

Cave des Vignerons de Buxy (Buxy) Behind the old business premises of this co-operative is a more recent cellar complex, where, among others, red Bourgogne Pinot Noir ages in oak casks. The firm is successful with its Montagny.

Bernard Michel (Saint-Vallerin) Small producer of, among others, Montagny Les Coères.

Château de la Saule This castle is situated at the end of the village of Montagny and is the property of Alain Roy-Thévenin.

An amusing painting on a wall in Buxy.

In the vicinity of the building are some old houses, some are even medieval. Just as the name suggests, *Montagny-lès-Buxy* is largely situated on a hill. The streets are narrow. The vineyards run from the village centre downwards into a broad valley. Just like Montagny, *Jully-lès-Buxy* offers a panorama across the area, while *Saint-Vallerin* has a Romanesque church. Slightly to the south of this wine village is the hamlet of *La Tour*, where the remains of an enormous medieval building can be seen.

RESTAURANT
Girardot
Buxy
✆ 85.92.04.04
Regional dishes are prepared (*poulet de Bresse aux morilles*) in a simple ambiance. Menus start at approx. FF 100. When the weather permits, you can eat outside at the rear.

His Montagny is delicious and one of the best of the entire *appellation*.
Veuve Steinmaier & Fils Various sorts of Montagny, with the Mont-Cuchot, which has a buttery taste, as the best.
Jean Vachet (Saint-Vallerin) Since 1959 this serious winegrower has, bit by bit, extended his estate and now produces wines with allure. One of these is the pure, generous Montagny Les Coères.

RELATED TO WINE
When it has at least 11.5% alcohol, Montagny may be sold as Montagny premier cru. This is the case with most wines.

MACONNAIS

At a certain point the wine districts of Chalonnais and Mâconnais merge indefinably with each other. However, there are still some clear differences, as is apparent by a visit to the most important wine districts, which are all situated east of the D 81. The landscape here is much more varied. There are forests, grain and vegetable fields and lush meadows in which Charolais cows quietly graze. Even more than Chalonnais, Mâconnais is a district of peaceful villages, whose silhouette is often determined by a Romanesque church. Romanesque architecture in Burgundy probably flowered first in Cluny, where the Benedictines had their headquarters.

The Mâconnais – named after the city of Mâcon which is just outside the wine area – has a somewhat softer climate than the more northern districts. The weather already seems to take on a Mediterranean character, which means that the grapes ripen a little earlier. The region has the shape of a bunch of grapes: broad at the top and narrow at the bottom. The most famous and most expensive wines are produced in the extreme south: the white Pouilly-Fuissé, Pouilly-Vinzelles, Pouilly-Loché and Saint-Véran. Red wine is also made elsewhere: Mâcon or Mâcon Supérieur (a little more alcohol). Generally, these are sympathetic wines from the gamay grape. The best sorts resemble a good Beaujolais. In quantity and quality, the red Mâcons are really overshadowed by the white. These have the chardonnay as a base and usually bear the *appellation* Mâcon-Villages or Mâcon plus a municipal name. This wine type is rather sturdy, often with fruity or floral aromas and a pleasing freshness – while the price remains reasonable.

The medieval castle of Brancion.

St-Huruge
Chau de la Serrée
Cimre Méroy
Grosne
Beugne
Bissy-s-U.
Uxelles
Balleure
Mancey
Robatot
St-Ythaire
Messeugne
Malay
Ougy
Lancharre
Nogent
Dulphey
Bierre
Montagny
les Chaumes
Bessuge
Collonge
Corcelle
Chau Sigy-le-Châtel
St-Hyppolite
Cortemblin
Chapaize
la Chapelle-sous-B.
Royer
Bonnay
Cormatin
Menh.
Brancion
Ozenay
C. de Beaufer
Besanceuil
Mont
Sailly
Cortevaix
C. de Brancion
Angoin
Confrançon
Chazelles
Lys
Prayes
Ft de Mortin
Martailly-lès-B.
Gratay
Plottes
Conflé
Salornay-s.-G.
Ameugny
Chissey-lès-Mâcon
Grevilly
Farges-lès-Mâcon
Chérizet
Mont
B. des Brûlées
le Bt Rameau
Taizé
Cruzille
Chardonnay
Champvent
Uchizy
Grosne
Culey
Bray
le Gros Chigy
Vitry-lès-Cluny
Flagy
Mont St-Romain
C. de la Pistole
Toury
Nouville
T. Orient.
Fissy
Pressy
Massy
Sirot
Massilly
Vivier
Grtes de Blanot
Charcuble
Mercey
Bezornay
Cortambert
Bissy-la-M.
Collongette
Montbellet
la Vineuse
Villard
Nogle
Sassy
Chau de Lourdon
Collonge
Chevagny
Blanot
Lugny
Bêne
Thurissey
St-Oyen
Donzy-le-National
Varanges
St-Gengoux-de-Scissé
Burgy
Mirande
Mt Epinet
Mt de la Péralle
Lournand
Mon
Bassy
Clapier
le Martray
Donzy-le-Pertuis
Viré
Grte d'Azé
Péronne
le Buc
Anc. Abbaye
Rizerolles
St Pierre de Lanques
Verizet
Fleurville
Quintaine
Reyssouze
Cluny
Château
Azé
Mt de Mandé
Mâcon-St-Albain
St-Albain
Ft des Trois Monts
Jalogny
Aine
St-Maurice-de-Satonnay
Clessé
Vernay
Mâcon-la-Salle
la Salle
Sanat.
Mouge
Domange
Boz
Senozan
Vaux
Pre Mouge
Vergesserin
Berzé-le-Châtel
Igé
Satonnay
Laizé
Chau
Ozan
Mazille
Chapelle-de-France
le Mont
Charbonnières
Asnières-s.-S.
Ste-Cécile
Verzé
Brandon
Grosne
St-Martin-Belle-Roche
Anc. Prieuré
Mt de la Fa
Blany
Péage
St-Jean-le-Priche
Bourgvilain
Corcelle
la Cre Blanche
Berzé-la-Ville
Clermain
Sologny
Perrière
Vésines
Manziat
Valouzin
Milly-Lamartine
Châtel de Lamartine
C. des Enceints
la Roche-Vineuse
Hurigny
Camp retranché
Chagny
St-Point
Bussières
Châl. de Montceau
les Thévelevs
Sancé
Dégotet
Limerol
les Cours
la Pierre de Fay
Pierreclos
Grd Bussières
Chevagny-lès-Chevrières
Salornay
Place-lès-Mâcon
Virolet
Feillens
Montillet
C. de Grd Vent
Prissé
Levigny
Fernant
les Roches
MÂCON
Replonges
Tramayes
Champvent
Serrières
Vergisson
Charnay-lès-M.
Hôtel-Dieu
le Creux
la Madeleine
758
la Farge
Roche de Solutré
Davayé
Sign. de la Mère Boitier
Gisement préhistorique
Solutré-Pouilly
Pont
St-Laurent-s.-S.
les Pugets
Pouilly
Grange du Bois
Chât. de St-Léger
Étg-Quinard
C. de Carcan
V. Château
Fuissé
Loché
la Croisée
Trades
Germolles-s.-G.
Crottet
Cenves
Chasselas
Vinzelles
Rontecolon
Varennes-lès-Mâcon
Chavannes
Leynes
St-Christophe
C. de Boutbon
Pruzilly
Chaintré
St-Vérand
Pont-de-Veyle
Péage
Villeneuve
St-Mamert
St-Jacques-des-Arrêts
le Vt Bourg
Grièges
C. de Fond Martin
Juillié
Mt de Bessay
Chânes
Crêches-s.-S.
Cormoranche-s.-Saône
St-Jean-s.-Veyle
Ouroux
Chlle
Juliénas
St-Amour-Bellevue
les Crêches
les Sablons
Laiz
Mgne des Eguillettes
Emeringes
les Ferrands
Jaillet
Cruzilles-lès-Mépillat
Bief de Malvert
Vauxrenard
Mauvaise
Chénas
les Leynards
Soleil
Saône
Bey
de Crie
C. du Fût d'Avenas
C. des Labourons
le Min à Vent
la Chapelle-de-Guinchay
les Bucheries
Garnerans
St André d'Huiriat
Avenas
C. de Durbize
Romanèche-Thorins
les Fargets
St-Symphorien
Bourchanin
Avanon
Mt Rochefort
T. Orient.
Fleurie
Crêches
St-Romain-des-Iles
Illiat
la Terrasse
Ardillats
Mgne d'Avenas
Chiroubles
Presle
Reclaine
la Mon Blanche
Thoissey
St-Didier-s.-Chalaronne
les Buantons
Lancié
Douby
Ardières
les Dépots
Beaujeu
Villié-Morgon
Corcelles-en-B.
Mon
Glenne
St-Didier-s.-Beaujeu
Lantignié
Dracé
Bge
Flurieux
St-Étienne
Dompierre
A 6-E 15-E 21
A 6-E 15
N 79
N 6
MÂCONNAIS

The undulating landscape of the Mâconnais.

Hotels

Auberge du Château
Cruzille
✆ 85.33.28.02
A simple hotel (six rooms starting at FF 150) with a restaurant where you can eat for under FF 100. Opened from Easter up to and including October.

Auberge du Vieux Brancion
Brancion
✆ 85.51.03.83
Near the castle. Six simple rooms (two with bath or shower) starting at about FF 170. The res-

The Wine Area of Macon and Macon-Villages

Most of the vineyards and villages of the Mâconnais are situated in an area that borders on the Chalonnais in the north, on the *autoroute* in the east, on the N 79 in the south and on the D 980 in the west. Within this rough rectangle runs the mountain chain of the Mâconnais; the city of Mâcon is situated just outside it. It is exceptionally enjoyable to explore this part of Burgundy because it has many beautiful parts, buildings and landscapes – not to speak of the (mainly white) wines.
The following route begins in the north, near

Recommended Producers

Auvigue-Burrier-Revel (Charnay-lès-Mâcon) Small wine merchant, specializing in white wines from the Mâconnais, in particular Saint-Véran and Pouilly-Fuissé. In general, the wines taste rather sturdy.

Domaine André Bonhomme (Viré) Pure, tasty Mâcon-Viré which usually undergoes cask ripening for six months.

Château des Cinq Tours (Viré) Beautiful Mâcon-Viré.

Collin et Bourisset (Crèches-sur-Saône) Among others, nice table wines. The interesting wines include two Moulin-à-Vents.

Cormatin (on the D 981). In this village there is a frequently visited 17th-century castle with six charmingly furnished rooms. Drive in an easterly direction to *Briançon*, a medieval hamlet. It is situated on a steep slope beside a fortress which was once one of the most important fortifications of southern Burgundy. The village – cars are forbidden – has 14th-century market halls as well as a Romanesque church with sublime frescos. Up to this point vineyards will scarcely have been seen. This changes near *Chardonnay.* This hamlet gave its name to the famous white grape variety. In 1988 it became one thousand years old. It has a 12th-century church and a 16th-century castle next to the wine co-operative. In the vicinity, there is a statue of a grape treader. The road now goes to *Uchizy*, a wine village with a strikingly large church, built by monks. By way of narrow, rustic roads you drive on to *Lugny.* On a hill above this village, the most important wine co-operative of Burgundy is situated, with a tasting and sales room. On Lugny's main street (south side) there is a big church (16th-century retable) and two round towers which are the remains of a 16th-century castle. Lugny is an excellent starting point for a small excursion, first to *Bissy-la-Mâconnaise*,

Clessé has a marvellous church.

taurant serves inexpensive regional dishes.

Hôtel du Centre
Lugny
✆ 85.33.22.82
Village hotel with both ordinary and chic rooms (10 rooms, starting at about FF 170), a bar and a restaurant: tasty dishes based on regional ingredients and excellent wines from the local co-operative, all for not much money. Very hospitable and

Co-operative Chardonnay (Chardonnay) The best, often crowned, wine is sold as Mâcon-Chardonnay.
Domaine de Chervin (Burgy) Mainly white Mâcon and Mâcon-Burgy. Both have a charming, soft-fresh taste.
Co-operative Charnay-lès-Mâcon (Charnay-lès-Mâcon) Saint-Véran is the speciality, but the Mâcon-Villages has just as much class.
Co-operative Clessé (Clessé) The wine most produced is the juicy, white Mâcon-Clessé, which is increasingly bottled by the co-operative itself.
Co-operative Igé Reliable, pure wines. Above all, the white Château London (a

There are two old castle towers in Lugny.

where, in the massive Romanesque church tower, there are wooden statuettes of saints to admire, and then to *Cruzille.* Just before this village, to the left of the road, the Musée des Outils d'Autrefois exhibits about 3500 tools from the past. Curzille also has a well-preserved 14th-century castle, where a medical institute is now situated. Now drive back to Lugny and then in the direction of Viré. The route runs past the hamlet of *Burgy,* with its 11th-century church and an extensive view. *Viré* consists of an elevated area, where there is a church with a pointed tower, and a lower area, with the co-operative, the Château des Cinq Tours (wine estate, 16th-century) and the village square where a statue of Bacchus stands. The *foyer rural* was built in the

The church of Uchizy.

friendly service. An address to note.
Château de Fleurville
Fleurville
✆ 85.33.12.17
Castle hotel with park, not far from the *route nationale*. 15 rooms (starting at around FF 430) and a good restaurant (menus start at about FF 150, with dishes such as *marmite de volaille de Bress*e). Swimming pool.
Château d'Igé
Igé
✆ 85.33.33.99
Luxurious accommodation with 12 spacious, finely furnished rooms and apartments (starting at around FF 500). The cuisine is of high quality. Menus start at FF 200.

Mâcon-Igé) and the ordinary Mâcon-Igé are worth tasting.
Co-operative Lugny (Lugny) Exemplary wines, in substantial quantities. A few delicious creations from the collection are the Crémant de Bourgogne, white Mâcon-Lugny Les Charmes, red Mâcon and Mâcon Supérieur and Bourgogne Passetoutgrains.
Co-operative Mancey (Mancey) The white wines, above all, demand attention here, such as the white Mâcon (Superieur) and Burgundy.
Co-operative Viré (Viré) Reliable quality. Much white Mâcon-Viré. The Crémant de Bourgogne is also tasty.

Statue near the church of Uchizy; it is called 'The Friends'.

Le Montagne de Brancion
Brancion
✆ 85.51.12.40
High on a hill in the vicinity of Brancion. Beautiful view from all 20 rooms (starting at about FF 400). They have been furnished with taste. Heated, outdoor swimming pool. A restaurant may be added.

Relais Lamartine
Bussières
✆ 85.36.64.71
Peacefully situated hotel with eight rooms (starting at about FF 360). You can eat breakfast and lunch outside. Menus start at about FF 100. A speciality is *parfait de foies de volaille aux baies de cassis.*

RESTAURANTS

Le Relais de Mâconnais
La Croix Blanche
✆ 85.36.60.72
The superb cuisine here attracts many guests. The menus start from a mere FF 135. Varied menu, with a regional accent (*aiguillettes de filet de Charolais au Mâcon rouge*). It is also a hotel.

direction of Vérizet, and has a library and a small wine museum next to it. By way of Quintaine, the route now goes to *Clessé.* The stainless steel tanks of the co-operative here contrast with the timeless little church, (11th-century). Driving in a

Domaine Goyard (Viré) Excellent white Mâcon-Viré.
Henri Lafarge (Bray) Unusually pleasant wines; a rather full, slightly nut-like white Mâcon as well as the red Mâcon-Bray and the Burgundy.
Domaine Manciat-Poncet (Lévigny) Wine fermented in stainless steel (Mâcon-Charnay) and small oak casks (Pouilly-Fuissé). Both are of excellent quality.
Mommessin (Charnay-lès-Mâcon) Wine merchant with a large range of wines, including the Côte d'Or (where it owns the Clos de Tart, in Morey-Saint-Denis), the Mâconnais and the Beaujolais. Wines

Wine can be tasted in Igé's chapel.

westerly direction, there are two routes to *Azé*. The northern road leads to Azé's prehistoric caves. Azé also has an archaeological museum, a Romanesque church and old market halls. It is worth the effort of driving from Azé to Cluny. The marvellous road runs past the charming village of *Donzy-le-Pertuis* (with an 11th-century church) and through the forests of *Cluny*. The Benedictine monastery, founded in Cluny in the 10th century, was, a century later, the most powerful in Europe. The model and the remains of the abbey church give an impression of the dimensions of the complex in its heyday. By taking either the D15 back to Azé or the narrower D 134, you proceed to *Igé*. The church clock tower bears the date 1975.

On the north side of Igé the 11th-century chapel of *Domange* is situated. During weekends and on holidays, the Musée de la Vigne, which is situated in the chapel, can be visited (also a wine tasting room). The route now goes southwards, to *Verzé*, which offers a panorama across southern

Monastery church of Cluny.

Relais de Montmartre
Viré
✆ 85.33.10.72
Well-cared-for inn on the village square. Stylish interior, nice service, regional cuisine. The menus begin under FF 100.

Saint-Pierre
Lugny
✆ 85.33.20.27
Simple restaurant. There is also a wine tasting room. Regional dishes and local wines adorn the menu. Wide panorama.

Le Wagon
Azé
✆ 85.33.30.97
You eat here in a train compartment with round tables. The menus – mainly regional dishes – begin under FF 100 and are prepared with care.

from very reasonable to good quality.
Domaine de Montbellet (Lugny) Delicious white Mâcon-Villages with a soft-fresh taste and often a hint of spices.
Domaine de Roally (Viré) Aromatic, variegated Mâcon-Viré of high quality. Minimal production.
Jean Signoret (Clessé).
Domaine Talmard (Uchizy) Above all, the white wines are impressive: Mâcon-Uchizy and Mâcon-Villages.
Jean Thévenet (Quintaine) White Mâcon-Clessé of impeccable quality and usually with a very fruity aroma.
Trénel Fils (Charnay-lès-Mâcon) The white as well as the red wines of the

Mâconnais. According to legend, the water of the village fountain can heal newborn babies. At Château d'Escolle (11th-century) partridges are bred for hunting. Descend to La Roche Vineuse, a thoroughfare along the N 79 and drive westward to *Berzé-la-Ville* with its Romanesque church and – just outside the village – La Chapelle aux Moines. This 11th- century building, in a small abbey, is famous for its rich wall paintings. Near the chapel there is also a beautiful view. Take the road downwards and turn right, in the direction of La Croix Blanche and then *Berzé-le-Châtel*. This hill village is dominated by a massive castle with 13 towers (12th to 15th century). Go back to La Croix Blanche and turn right to *Milly-Lamartine*, where Alphonse de Lamartine (see also Mâcon) spent his youth. The village honours him with a bust. There is also a Romanesque church. It is not far from here to *Pierreclos* with its 14th-century castle, which houses, among other things two museums (devoted to bread and wine), a 12th-century chapel and enormous hearths. This is the end of the route.

The 14th-century castle of Pierreclos.

Tourist Tips

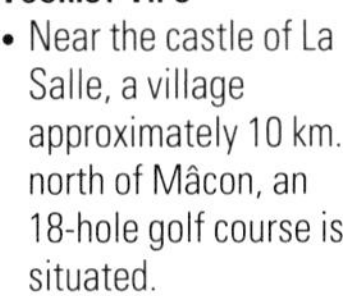

- Near the castle of La Salle, a village approximately 10 km. north of Mâcon, an 18-hole golf course is situated.
- In the Château de Pierreclos there is a wax statue of Lamartine. It was made by the Musée Grevin in Paris.

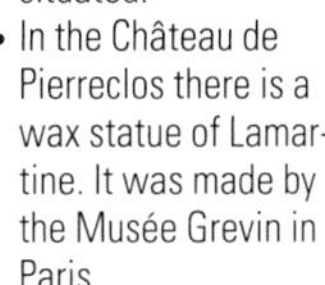

- Goat cheese is served everywhere in the Mâconnais and in all possible ways.
- In the hamlet of Eau-Vive, near La Roche Vineuse, the open air museum Au Bout de Monde is situated, with houses from various cultures.

business are firm and rich in fruit. Especially fine creations, such as the Mâcon-Villages, Saint-Véran, Pouilly-Fuissé, crus from Beaujolais and red Mâcon.

Related to Wine

- In Mâconnais around 90% of the wine is made by co-operatives.
- During the second half of May, one of France's largest wine exchanges takes place annually in Mâcon.
- In Créches-sur-Saône, along the N 6, is the Cellier-Expo, where information about wine can be found.
- During Palm Sunday weekend Lugny usually organizes a wine exchange.

MACON

Just like Chalon-sur-Saône, Mâcon, which has approximately 40,000 inhabitants, is situated along the Saône and was an important settlement in Roman times. In many workshops at that time, spears and arrows were made, for soldiers as well as for hunters. In those days winegrowing was already practised around Mâcon; a fact that is mentioned by the poet Ausonius.

Mâcon's places of interest are mainly found in the old centre, along the Saône. There is a car park for 500 cars. Amid the tin and chrome rises the statue of Alphonse de Lamartine (1790-1869). This poet and politician was born in Mâcon, a fact that is constantly brought to the visitor's attention. A street, a quay and a promenade have been named after him, while, in the Hôtel Senecé (rue Sigorne), a museum has been devoted to him. You can also see a life-size Lamartine surrounded by other personages in an enormous mosaic on a side wall (corner of rue Gambetta and rue Edouard-Herriot). On the quay, close to the statue of the famous citizen, is the Hôtel Montrevel, an imposing, palatial building from the 18th century. Nowadays it functions as the city hall. Directly behind it there is a cosy shopping street and the strikingly designed Office du Tourisme. Here you can ask about entrance to the chapel of the Résidence Soufflot, a former hospital, which is situated nearby. The chapel has a striking oval shape. In the small tower to the right of the gateway is a sort of hatch through which unwished-

City hall with the statue of Lamartine in front.

Flower booth on the place aux Herbes.

for babies could be discreetly handed over to the hospital. Across from the Office du Tourisme is the Neo-Romanesque church of Saint-Pierre with its elegant, pointed towers. By following the shopping street in a northerly direction, you arrive at the place aux Herbes, with the Maison de Bois on a corner. This is the oldest building of Mâcon – and the most famous. It was built around 1500. On the wooden façade there are numerous small sculptures of people and animals in all sorts of unusual situations. After walking to the end of the shopping street, you reach the Vieux Saint-Vincent. This is a former cathedral which was repeatedly destroyed and of which little now remains other than two, unequal, octagonal towers. Now walk further in a westerly direction, until you come to the Musée des Ursulines, where historic objects and works of art have been collected. The oldest date from the prehistoric age and were found near Solutré (see Pouilly-Fuissé). The glass windows and ceramics also deserve attention.

The Neo-Romanesque Saint-Pierre.

Not far from the museum is the Neo-Classical cathedral of Saint-Vincent. It was built by the Parisian Guy de Gisors and commissioned by Napoleon, which is why the church was initially called Saint-Napoléon. After the departure of the emperor, the building was baptised Saint-Louis (in hommage to Louis XVIII) but when Napoleon returned from Elba the neutral name of Saint-Vincent was chosen to avoid any further confusion. The Hôtel-Dieu, which is situated in the vicinity, was built in the 18th century and carries a sizeable, elliptical dome. On the ground floor a drug store can be visited, containing a fine collection of pots from the time of Louis XV. Slightly to the north of Mâcon's old centre, in a green area, the *Maison Mâconnaise des Vins* (484 avenue de Lattre-de-Tassigny) is situated. It sells wines from Mâconnais and northerly Beaujolais, while the large room is furnished as a simple restaurant.

HOTEL
La Vigne Blanche
Fuissé
✆ 85.35.60.50
A dozen pleasant, two-star rooms (starting at about FF 200). In the rustic, unpretentious restaurant, you can eat Burgundian dishes such as frog's legs and *coq au vin*; a few of the regional wines are served by the glass. The menus begin under FF 100.

RESTAURANTS
Chez Cantal
Vergisson
✆ 85.35.84.69
Simple establishment. Serves only a plat du jour. Small terrace, across from the church.
Le Petit Trou
Vinzelles
✆ 85.35.60.24
In the dining room a very inexpensive menu of the day is offered. It is also a café.
Au Pouilly-Fuissé
Fuissé
✆ 85.35.60.68
The new owners have given this pleasant business a new look. In the light interior you can enjoy honest, tasty, regional dishes such as *mousseline de brochet à la crème de cèpes, pou-*

Château Fuissé in the village of the same name.

POUILLY-FUISSE

There is no doubt that Pouilly-Fuissé is the most famous wine from the Mâconnais – and also the most expensive. This white Burgundy's place of origin is straight to the west of the city of Mâcon and can be recognized from a distance by two steeply rising rocks, which, like the petrified bows of ships, seem to cut through a stormy sea of green grapevines. These are the cliffs of Vergisson and Solutré. Coming from Pierreclos (-Mâcon and Mâcon-Villages) or Davayé (Saint-Véran), *Vergisson* is the first village to visit. It is small and consists of sloping streets. High above the pointed church spire towers a steep cliff. Parts of it are ochre and pink in colour. A cave has been found near the cliff containing the remains of a Neanderthal man. In the hamlet of *Chancerons*, on the south side of Vergisson, stands a three-metre-high menhir. From Vergisson a nar-

RECOMMENDED PRODUCERS
Château de Beauregard (Fuissé) Important estate which produces distinguished wines, fermented in wooden casks.
Cave des Grands Crus Blancs (Vinzelles) For Pouilly-Vinzelles and Pouilly-Loché.
Louis Curveux (Fuissé) Excellent.
Château Fuissé (Fuissé) Superb Pouilly-Fuissé Vieilles Vignes. The other wines from this eminent estate also have a lot of quality: Saint-Véran, Morgon Charmes, etc.
Roger Duboeuf & Fils (Chaintré) In the 16th-century tasting room visitors can discover delicious wines, including white

row, winding road runs via wooded slopes to *Solutré.* The cliff above it is even more impressive than that of Vergisson. On this rock, the Gallic leader Vercingetorix lit a fire in order to can the tribes together for a struggle for independence. This is remembered annually with a large bonfire on the same spot on Saint John's day. A prehistoric hunting camp was found at the foot of the rock in 1866. Between 35,000 and 10,000 BC, thousands of horses and reindeer were driven here, to be slaughtered. Excavations have resulted in one of Europe's richest collections of objects from prehistoric times. This has, for a large part, been brought together in the Musée Départemental de Préhistoire, at the foot of the rock. Aside from hunting tools, the museum, which was opened in 1987, also has statuettes, including a small, primitive sculpture of a mammoth. Solutré itself is a charming village. In the *Caveau Pouilly-Fuissé* you can taste the local wine (for a fee) and also buy bottles of it. Diagonally opposite stand the church (Romanesque, 12th-century) and La Bou-

let rôti à la fleur de thym or *andouillette braisée à la moutarde.* This is the best place to eat in the district. A weekday menu of less than FF 100. The ordinary menus begin at about FF 115.

In Fuissé there is a large route sign.

Tourist Tips

- It is possible to ascend the cliff of Solutré by way of a footpath – or as a mountaineer.
- On a hill near Solutré the hamlet of La Grange du Bois is located. There is a 12th-century monastery and a walking route has been laid out. The view is fabulous. You can eat in the rustic *Auberge de la Grange du Bois*, mainly *grillades* (tel. 85.37.80.78).

Visitors are welcome.

tique, a store selling wine, wine articles, jewellery, ceramics and other items. By driving from Solutré to Fuissé, you go through the hamlet of *Pouilly*. In the elevated village area (fine view) there is a chapel from the 15th century and a castle, flanked by towers, which dates from the 16th century. *Fuissé* was built in a natural amphitheatre, most of the slopes of which are planted with grapevines. The isolated Neo-Gothic church (1872) has an allegorical depiction of the struggle against the plant-lice *Phylloxera* above its entrance. In the village centre is a rather dilapidated Romanesque church. From Fuissé, a winding road runs to the last municipality of the *appellation* Pouilly-Fuissé, *Chaintré*. On a wall near the church is a splendid, colourful wall painting, while a large bottle, bearing the names of winegrowers,

Beaujolais and Pouilly-Fuissé.

Domaine Guffens-Heynen (Vergisson) The Belgian owner Jean-Marie Guffens has a striking personality and makes a small number of high-quality wines: Pouilly-Fuissé and white and red Mâcon-Pierreclos.

Also Recommended André Besson (Pouilly), Co-operative Chaintré (Chaintré), Dom. Cordier Père & Fils (Fuissé), Dom. Corsin (Fuissé), J.A. Ferret (Fuissé), André Forest (Vergisson), Dom. des Granges (Chaintré), René Guérin (Vergisson), Jean Lacoste (Fuissé), Roger Luquet (Fuissé), Dom. Mathias (Chaintré), Gilles Noblet (Fuissé), René Perraton (Chaintré), Roger

reminds one once more that this is a wine village. While a good Pouilly-Fuissé is a rich white wine that gives impressions of fruit, flowers, nuts and also often of wood plus vanilla, there are two wines that have slightly less quality – but cost much less. These are Pouilly-Vinzelles and Pouilly-Loché. Unfortunately, both of them are hard to find: they do not make up even one-tenth of the volume of Pouilly-Fuissé. The birth-place of Pouilly-Vinzelles is the village of *Vinzelles*. A few castle-like buildings are found there; a white statue of the Virgin Mary decorates the partially 12th- century, partially 17th-century church. *Loché*, from where Pouilly-Loché originates, enjoys fame mainly because of its TGV station. Near the Romanesque village church, with its octagonal, narrow tower, there is a beautiful, covered portal. The local castle (13th to 18th century) has made its own wine since 1989, but the quality is variable. The Château de Loché can be visited by appointment only.

The rock of Vergisson.

Saumaize (Vergisson), Dom. le Val des Roches (Vergisson).

Restaurants

Au Fin Bec
Leynes
✆ 85.35.11.77
It usually smells very appetising when you enter. The owner of this pleasant restaurant is also the cook. The cuisine is regional. Various menus for less than FF 100.

Relais Beaujolais-Mâconnais
Leynes
✆ 85.35.11.29
Simple, regional dishes and regional wines. The menus begin under FF 100.

Wall decoration with trompe l'oeil in Davayé.

Saint-Veran

The *appellation* is closely tied in with that of Pouilly-Fuissé. It consists of six bordering municipalities (plus parts of Solutré and Saint-Amour-Bellevue). Formerly they produced Mâcon-Villages or white Beaujolais. As a wine, the – always white – Saint-Véran is usually somewhat slimmer and less rich in dimension than Pouilly-Fuissé. There are exceptions though: a superior Saint-Véran can have more to offer than an average Pouilly-Fuissé.

The northern municipality is *Prissé.* On a façade on the main street there is a large wall painting in trompe-l'oeil. There are two castles in this village (they cannot be visited): Manoir de la Cerve (15th/16th century) and Château

Saint-Vérand in the heart of Saint-Véran.

Recommended Producers

Domaine des Pérelles (Chânes) This estate is run by André Larochette and produces, among others, a successful Saint-Véran.

Cooperative Prissé (Prissé) Modern equipped business that lets its fine white wines ferment in stainless steel tanks: Saint-Véran, Mâcon-Villages and Bourgogne Aligoté.

Domaine des Pierres Rouges (Chasselas) This average-sized estate enjoys a good name because of, among others, its quite generous, soft-fresh Saint-Véran. The estate is run by the Marcel family.

Domaine des Valanges (Davayé) A deli-

de Monceau (17th century). The poet Bauderon lived in the first, and in the second Lamartine. On a hill, neighbouring *Davayé* has a Romanesque church dating from the 12th century, an old bathing place, a couple of castles, a contemporary fresco on the wall of the co-operative and a well-known school of winegrowing.

Church gable in Davayé.

To the south of Chaintré, the rather uninteresting village of Chânes is situated. *Saint-Vérand* is a medieval hill village with a beautifully restored small church from the 12th and 15th centuries. Take a look at the fresco inside. The village was formerly called Saint-Véran-des-Vignes. Against a hill near *Leynes* stand the remains of a castle and a monastery. The church near the spacious, sloping village square is one of the few 16th-century churches in Burgundy. *Chasselas* gave its name to a table and wine grape. In the village there is a small Romanesque church and, on the outskirts, a large, attractive castle, which is, in part, 14th-century. The sixth village is *Chânes.*

The church of Saint-Vérand.

Le Tire Bouchon
Saint-Vérand
✆ 85.37.15.33
Property of a winegrowing family. *Coq au Beaujolais Villages, entrecôte charolaise* and similar dishes. Menus start at less than FF 100. Situated at the foot of the village.

Tourist Tip

Next to the church of Saint-Vérand is a striking wooden fountain. It was given to the village in 1992 by France's highest town, Saint-Véran (Queraz).

cious, complete Saint-Véran is made here, which is expressive in aroma and taste. The owner is called Michel Paquet. **Also Recommended** Georges Chagny/-Domaine la Maison (Leynes), Henri-Lucius Grégoire (Davayé), Jean-Jacques Martin (Chânes), Maurice Martin (Davayé).

Related to Wine

On a hill behind the old church of Davayé stands the angular complex of the Lycée Viticole de Davayé. Young winegrowers are taught here. It also makes wine from its own vineyards, including a Saint-Véran.

Beaujolais

With more than half of the total number of vineyards, Beaujolais is by far the largest of the five Burgundian districts. Wine grapes are lord and master here, in particular the blue gamay, the only accepted variety for red (and rosé) wines in this area. A certain amount of white Beaujolais is also made, based on the chardonnay. The best and most powerful wines of Beaujolais are the ten so-called crus. These come from villages or groups of villages in the northern part of the area. These are, from north to south, Saint-Amour, Juliénas, Chénas, Moulin-à-Vent, Fleurie, Chiroubles, Morgon, Régnié, Brouilly and Côte de Brouilly. The wines from Beaujolais-Villages are somewhat simpler. Their areas of production are approximately 40 villages, most of which are situated in the north. Finally, there is Beaujolais and Beaujolais Supérieur (with somewhat more alcohol). A special version of Beaujolais and Beaujolais-Villages is offered annually as Beaujolais Primeur or Beaujolais Nouveau. This is fermented in such a way that the fruit of the grape is kept optimally in the wine. Beaujolais Primeur tastes best in its earliest youth and is sold from the third Thursday in November. Fruit is characteristic of all the red Beaujolais sorts, above all that of small red berries and fruits (strawberries, raspberries, cherries). Serve Beaujolais chilled: about 16 degrees (Celsius) is ideal.

Wine and tourist information.

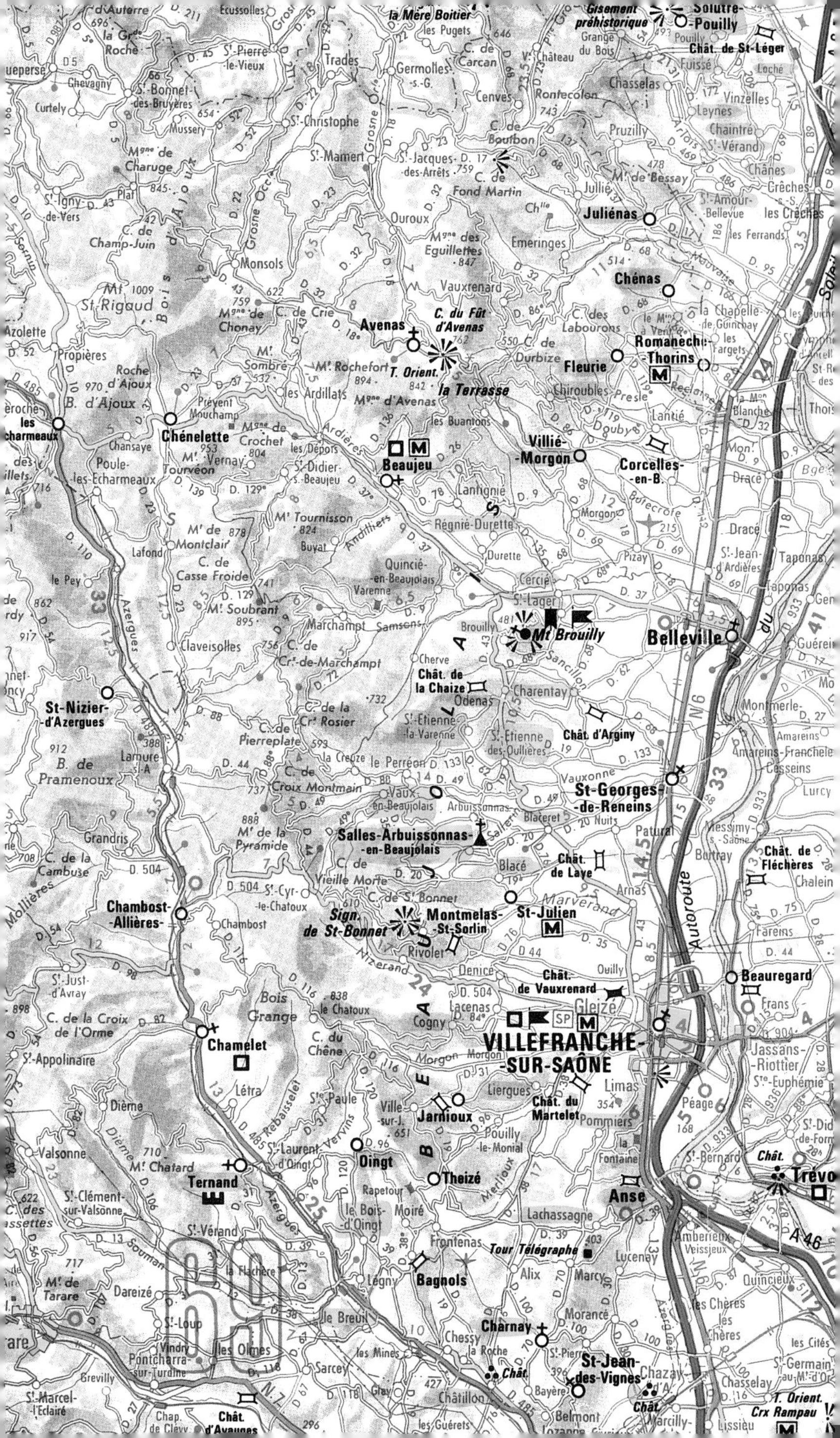

Saint-Amour

The northernmost cru of Beaujolais, Saint-Amour, derives its name from the district of Saint-Amour-Bellevue, which is made up of isolated suburbs. Le Bourg, with its Romanesque village church (12th-century retable), is situated on a hill top. From Le Bourg the road runs by way of vineyards to Platre-Durand. This consists mainly of a large square with two restaurants and a wine tasting room. A statue of a Roman legionary, near the reception hall of Saint-Amour-Bellevue, is witness to the legend that a soldier/martyr, called Amor(e) or Amator, settled here at the end of the 3rd century, after having been converted to Catholicism. The wine type Saint-Amour is often just as sweet as his name suggests: fruity, charming and sometimes almost like satin in structure.

Restaurants
Auberge du Paradis
✆ 85.37.10.26
Village inn where large groups are welcomed. Various menus under FF 100 with regional dishes such as *la volaille à la beaujolaise* and *guenelle de brochet* with *sauce Nantua.*
Chez Jean-Pierre
✆ 85.37.41.26
Diagonally across from its competitor, on the same square. The business is somewhat smaller and the prices somewhat higher – but for around FF 100 there is still a three-course menu of the day.

The Romanesque village church.

Dining in paradise.

Tourist Tip
Above the suburb of La Ville, stands the Château de Saint-Amour.

Recommended Producers
Domaine des Ducs Charming wines.
Francis Saillant Attractive tasting cellar.
Also Recommended Dom. de la Cave Lamartine, André Poitevin, Georges Spay, Georges Trichard.

Related to Wine
- The Coupe Dailly is awarded annually for the best Saint-Amour. Louis Dailly gained recognition in 1946 for the title of origin Saint-Amour.
- The wine festival takes place on July 1.
- The wine tasting room is open during weekends and on holidays.

A choice of restaurants.

JULIENAS

That Juliénas is a wine village is immediately clear to visitors who park their cars on the place du Marché because not only is there a store dealing in wine cellar materials (and articles for the home) but there is also a store owned by winegrower Pierre Perrachon (from Chénas) and a strikingly designed restaurant with the name of *Le Coq au Vin.* If there should still be doubts then a walk

A view across Juliénas.

HOTEL

Hôtel des Vignes
✆ 74.04.43.70
This two-star hotel is peacefully situated on the road between Saint-Amour (La Ville) and Juliénas. It has 20 pleasant rooms, prices starting at FF 235.

RESTAURANTS

Le Coq au Vin
✆ 74.04.41.98
Not only do the façade and interior command respect, but also the cuisine of this stylish bistro, because the dishes here (such as *poularde de Bresse à la crème*) have taste and character. Menus start

RECOMMENDED PRODUCERS

Domaine de la Boittiére Hefty Juliénas.

Jean Buiron A sometimes surprisingly subtle, complete Juliénas is produced here.

Domaine des Chers The Juliénas from this estate – owner Jacques Briday – not only has fruit but also ripening potential.

Co-operative Juliénas In 1992 a new, modern cellar complex was built next to the Château du Bois de la Salle, where this *cave co-operative* has its tasting room. Their own Juliénas is usually sturdy in structure and reliable in quality.

Château de Juliénas Extremely large

An old church turned wine premises.

in the direction of the church will dispel them because, across from the present-day church with its high, pointed tower, is the old church – which has functioned since 1954 as a wine tasting room. This *Cellier de la Vieille Eglise* has bacchanalian depictions on its inside walls and attracts many people at the weekend. The origins of this wine village apparently date back to Roman times. Perhaps the name Juliénas is derived from Julius Caesar – but this is also said to be the case for neighbouring Jullié (the vineyards of which belong to the *appellation* Juliénas).

One of the oldest local buildings is the Château de Juliénas, situated just outside the village centre. It has impressive cellars. Further along the same road is the Maison de la Dîme, a tollhouse from the 16th century. Juliénas also has an important wine co-operative. It is situated at the foot of the village and has equipped the top floor of the 17th-century Château du Bois de la Salle as a tasting room.

The 'new church'.

at around FF 100. Behind the dining room there is a small terrace.

Ma Petite Auberge
✆ 74.04.49.29
Situated next to *Le Coq au Vin*. The menus begin under FF 100 and are regional in character. Also a simple hotel called *Chez la Rose* with a dozen rooms.

Tourist Tip
There is a nice little store, Le Sarment, situated between the square and the church. It sells bric-a-brac and wine articles.

estate which only bottles part of the harvest itself. The wine is generally fruity and more than correct. The castle certainly deserves a visit, if only for its magnificent cellars.
Jean-Marc Monnet Excellent.
Also Recommended Domaine des Fouillouses.

Related to Wine
On the second Sunday of November, Juliénas celebrates the festival of the new wine. An award is then given to the person who has been most positive in expressing himself about wine (preferably Juliénas). The award consists of 104 bottles of Juliénas: two for each weekend.

Chenas

Chénas is not only the smallest of the crus, but also the most confusing, because many of the vineyards in the municipality of the same name give Moulin-à-Vent, while neighbouring La Chapelle-de-Guinchay produces twice as much Chénas as Chénas itself.
The village consists of a few isolated, small suburbs in the midst of hilly vineyards. The centre of the village is marked by a large, grey church. The Château de Chénas is not very attractive from the outside, but has large, vaulted cellars. These are used by the local *cave coopérative*, which owns the castle and has placed modern industrial buildings next to it. Worked casks can be seen in the tasting room of the co-operative. As a wine, Chénas is almost as powerful as Moulin-à-Vent and ageing for a few years often does it good. Locally, it is called 'a bouquet of flowers in a basket of velvet'.

Restaurant
Robin/Relais des Grands Crus
✆ 85.36.72.67
This is one of the best places to eat in Beaujolais. *Patron* Daniel Robin prepares tasty regional dishes of high quality. His *salade beaujolaise* is, in itself, worth the detour and the same goes for the *poulet de Bresse rôti au four.* Menus start at about FF 200.

Tourist Tip
The name *Chénas* comes from *chêne*, meaning oak, because there was once a large forest of oak trees here. The trees were cut down centuries ago.°

The church stands in the midst of grapevines.

Recommended Producers
Château Bonnet (La Chapelle-de-Guinchay) In this castle the Perrachon family make three good wines, of which the firm Chénas, full of fruit, is generally the best.
Domaine des Brureaux A Chénas is produced here which can, without difficulty, age for three years or longer. The same family runs the *Robin* restaurant.
Domaine Champagnon Superior Chénas.
Co-operative Chénas This large firm ships almost 40% of all Chénas.
Also Recommended Hubert Lapierre (La Chapelle-de-Guinchay).

Moulin-a-Vent

The structure after which the cru Moulin-à-Vent is named is an ancient, vaneless grain mill from the 13th century. It is situated on a hill between the villages of Romanèche-Thorins (to which municipality it belongs) and Chénas. In the direct vicinity of the monument are the official wine tasting room of Moulin-à-Vent and a few wine estates, including two small castles. Nowadays the view from the mill reveals a sea of grapevines. Formerly this was not the case because grain was mainly grown in Romanèche-Thorins at one time. The name Romanèche comes from Romana Esca: grain depot of the Roman legions. The title of origin, Moulin-à-Vent, encompasses the municipality of Romanèche-Thorins as well as approximately three-quarters of Chénas. Particularly in Romanèche-Thorins, the visitor is regularly reminded of the name of the local wine because there are small windmills in many gardens. The wine is among the best of Beaujolais, thanks to a dark colour and a generous taste with a soft fruitiness and sufficient tannin to ripen for a few years. Moulin-à-Vent, together with Côte de

To the right is the windmill after which Moulin-à-Vent is named.

Hotel
Les Maritonnes
✆ 85.35.51.70
The 20 rooms of this hotel, which is surrounded by a park, are stylishly furnished and supplied with all comforts. Double-glazing ensures that the nearby highway does not cause any disturbance. Prices start at about FF 400. The restaurant also deserves a recommendation. It is spacious, candles burn, waitresses offer friendly service, the wine selection is wide, but the Réserve Maison can be trusted blindly and the regional cuisine is extremely good. Menus start at approx. FF 200.

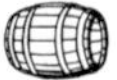

Recommended Producers
Domaine de la Bruyière
Georges Duboeuf Since 1964, Georges Duboeuf has worked himself up from bottler to the biggest wine merchant of Beaujolais. Distinctive of all Duboeuf wines is a strong fruitiness.
Château des Jacques Perfectly maintained estate with a few dozen hectares of vineyards. It produces two high-quality wines, a strong Moulin-â-Vent and a likewise superior white Beaujolais, the Grand Clos de Loyse.
Jacky Janodet Strong wines (such as Moulin-à-Vent and Morgon) which can easily be set aside for a few years.

Near the local tasting premises.

Brouilly and Chénas, is also one of the most powerful wines that the region produces. The Musée Guillon in Romanèche-Thorins is a place of interest. It contains about 100 models of wooden towers, which were made by the French guild of carpenters (Compagnons Charpentiers du Tour de France). On the square, by the large church, there is a bust of Benoît Raclet (1780-1844). In the first half of the last century he discovered a remedy against the pyrale, a small worm that destroys the grape leaves. The remedy is simply hot water. As the saviour of the vineyard, Raclet is honoured annually during the Fête Raclet. This takes place on the last Saturday of October. Raclet's house has been set up as a museum.

The centre of Romanèche-Thorins.

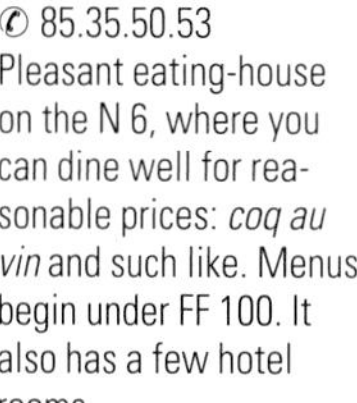

Restaurant
La Maison Blanche
✆ 85.35.50.53
Pleasant eating-house on the N 6, where you can dine well for reasonable prices: *coq au vin* and such like. Menus begin under FF 100. It also has a few hotel rooms.

Tourist Tip

- Touroparc is situated in La Maison Blanche (along the N 6) near Romanèche-Thorins. It houses a large zoo with more than 300 species of animals from five continents. Touroparc is also an amusement park with a swimming pool, roller coaster, miniature train, cave boat trip and other attractions.
- By way of Lancié, it is not far to Château de Corcelles, a marvellously maintained, 15th-century monument which can be visited (not on Sundays and public holidays) and is the heart of a wine estate.

Jean Mortet The Moulin-à-Vents from this winegrower are always wood-matured and strong and fruity at the same time. The best is usually Les Rouchaux.
Château du Moulin-à-Vent This castle, which is close to the old grain mill, is the heart of a large wine estate, where a generous, fine Moulin-à-Vent of the highest quality is produced. It always undergoes maturing in oak casks.
Michel Gaidon Pahud-Gaidon At Château Portier (in the vicinity of the mill) various wines are produced, including an unusually successful Moulin-à-Vent: the Cuvée Château-Portier, originating from old vines.

HOTEL

Les Grands Vins
✆ 74.69.81.43
Modern, well-run hotel just outside of the village centre, with 20 reasonably comfortable rooms (starting at about FF 300). Peace is guaranteed. Small swimming pool.

RESTAURANTS

Auberge du Cep
✆ 74.04.10.77
At the corner of the church square. Cuisine of high quality, inventive as well as regional. High prices: the most inexpensive menu costs about FF 300.

Restaurant des Sports
✆ 74.04.12.69
Church square. Regional dishes, including *coq au vin*, are served inexpensively (FF 100 and less).

TOURIST TIPS

- On Saturday mornings there is a market on the church square.
- Across from the church there is a store selling wine articles and wines: La Cave Vigneronne.
- A beautiful road runs between Chénas and Fleurie.

Colourful wall near the wine co-operative.

FLEURIE

In the winegrowing village of Fleurie, one of the largest selling crus of the Beaujolais is made. A good Fleurie has a playful, juicy taste with an elegant firmness and a seductive aroma of red berries and fruits and spring flowers. Fleurie is generally a peaceful village. Life takes place, for the most part, on the village square (19th-century church) where the stores, cafes and restaurants are concentrated. On the west side of Fleurie a large hill rises, with a chapel on top. On the first weekend after November 1 (All Saints' Day), peace is broken because a large wine exchange then takes place here, with wines from Beaujolais, Mâconnais and Chalonnais: Fleurie is then visited by thousands of winegrowers, wine lovers and wine merchants.

RECOMMENDED PRODUCERS

Domaine Bernard Exemplary Fleurie.
René Berrod/Les Roches du Vivier Quality shines through in two of the three wines that the Berrod family produce: the Fleurie and the Moulin-à-Vent.
Co-operative Fleurie This is a very large firm which sells the majority of its wines in bulk to wine merchants. Apart from Fleurie five other wines are produced.
Michel Chignard Crowned wines.
Michel Tribolet Aromatic Fleurie.
Also Recommended Dom. de la Grand'Cour, Chât. des Labourons, Dom. du Point du Jour.

Left to the tasting chalet.

Chiroubles

Coming from Fleurie, the exit for Chiroubles is clearly in dicated. This small village – home to the cru of the same name – is situated at a height of 400 metres and has a small, 19th-century church with a dome that looks Byzantine. Next to it is a bust of Victor Pulliat, the brilliant researcher who found a remedy against the gluttonous grape aphid *Phylloxera*: grafting on American stalks. The co-operative – with tasting room – is situated nearby. The municipality also has a tasting room, in a chalet high above the village. You can eat well here – and enjoy a panoramic view.

Of all the crus, Chiroubles is usually the most delicate and light-footed. Normally you must wait to drink it because it tastes best a year after its harvest.

The highest situated wine village.

Restaurant

Chez Marc et Annick

✆ 74.04.24.87

Pleasant inn in the middle of the village. For less than FF 100 you can eat delicious dishes, for example, *coq au vin* or *entrecôte au Chiroubles.*

Tourist Tips

- The municipal tasting room, which is situated high on a mountain, is called La Terrasse du Beaujolais. It would be wise to call first (tel. 74.04.20.79) to see if it is open. In the afternoon you can have tea and cakes.
- The tiny chapel of Saint-Roch, dating from the 17th century, is more beautiful than the local church.

Recommended Producers

Domaine Bouillard
Domaine Cheysson-les-Farges
Domaine du Clos Verdy
Domaine de la Combe aux Loups
André Depré
Bernard Méziat
Alain Passot/Dom. de la Grosse Pierre
Château de Raousset
Francis Tomatis & Fils.

Related to Wine

Every April, Chiroubles holds the Fête des Crus, including a wine competition; the winner receives the Coupe Victor Pulliat.

Morgon

In 1867 the villages of Villié and Morgon became one municipality. Since then the border has been at Mont du Py, the 352-metre-high remains of a volcano, with Villié on the north side of the hill and Morgon on the south side. Mont du Py – like the Charmes – is one of the best vineyards of the *appellation* Morgon. It has very aptly been said of Morgon's wine that it has: 'Le fruit d'un Beaujolais, le charme d'un Bourgogne'. Apart from this, a characteristic wine from this cru is distinguished by its aroma of wild cherries and by a certain 'mustiness', which is a result of its special bottom (the *roche pourrie*, decayed rock). The wine tasting room of Morgon is one of the most visited of the region. It is housed in the vaulted cellars of a castle near the village centre; in front of it is a park.

Hotels

Château du Pizay
Pizay
✆ 74.66.51.41
This castle-hotel (with a decorative garden) has modern, tastefully decorated rooms (about 60, starting at around FF 550). In the vaulted dining room, cleverly prepared dishes with a regional touch are served. Menus start at approx. FF 200. Swimming pool. It is also a wine estate.

Le Villon
✆ 74.69.16.16
Hotel with 45 rather spacious rooms (starting at about FF 375). Adequate bathroom facilities. In the restaurant you can order various Morgons with dishes such as *coq au vin* and *filet de porc au vin rouge*. Menus start at about FF 100. Swimming pool.

Restaurant

Le Relais des Caveaux
✆ 74.02.21.77
Good meals at reasonable prices (starting at about FF 100).

There is a tasting room under the castle.

Recommended Producers

Domaine de la Chanaise Exemplary.
Domaine du Coteau des Lys Fleshy Morgons.
Louis Claude Desvignes Three Morgons.
Georges Passot This wine maker has been proclaimed the best of Morgon.
Jacky Passot Morgons with distinction.
Château de Pizay (Pizay) Elegant, pure wine with small red fruits.
Domaine Savoye Morgon Côte du Py.
Also Recommended Bernard Botteron, Joseph Chamonard, Dom. du Colonat, Dom. Goy, Dom. des Pillets, Dom. de Ruyère.

A pleasant place to eat.

Regnie

Régnié has been the tenth cru of Beaujolais since 1988. The wine is colourful, expressive, very fruity and fairly firm. The most notable building in Régnié-Durette) is the church with two towers. Not far away is the tasting room. Outside the village centre is the Domaine de la Grange-Charton. This is the property of the Hospices de Beaujeu and consists of an enormous courtyard, surrounded by houses and cellars. There are two castles near the village: Château de la Pierre and Château des Vergers.

The impressive church of Régnié-Durette.

Restaurants

Auberge la Vigneronne
✆ 74.04.35.95
Rustic, country restaurant. Inexpensive menus (under FF 100) with dishes such as *saucisson au Régnié* and *coq au Régnié*. Next to the wine tasting room.

Le Pied de Vigne
✆ 74.04.31.01
This inn was recently renovated with taste. Flowery interior. Well-priced regional dishes (*volaille fermière au Régnié*) in menus costing less than FF 100. When this guide appears, the hotel will probably be finished; it will have 36 rooms.

Tourist Tips

- At the end of October there is a bicycle race for ex-professionals, Le Grand Prix des Retrouvailles.
- Famous chansonniers perform almost annually in Régnié during the Night of the Wine.
- There is a fine road between Régnié and Lantigné.

Recommended Producers

Domaine des Braves The owner is a great bicycle race enthusiast.
Desplace Frères/Domaine du Crêt des Bruyères Pure Régnié with good fruit.
Also Recommended Jean et Yves Durand/Dom. de Ponchon, Dom. de la

Gérarde, Michel Rampon Père & Fils, Joël Rochette, Domaine de la Roze.

Related to Wine

The wines from the Domaine de la Grange-Charton are sold during the auction of the Hospices de Beaujeu, on the second Sunday of December.

Château de la Chaize in Odenas.

Hotels

Le Mont Brouilly
Quincié-en-Beaujolais
✆ 74.04.33.73
In the suburb of Le Pont des Samsons, a short distance from the D 37. It has about 30 pleasant rooms (about FF 300). Those at the rear are the most peaceful and offer a view of Mont Brouilly. In the restaurant you can eat *tournedos au Brouilly, coq au Beaujolais* and other regional dishes. Menus start at FF 100.

La Vigne et Les Vins
Quincié-en-Beaujolais
✆ 74.04.32.40

Brouilly and Cote de Brouilly

The entrance to southern Beaujolais is dominated by the 483-metre-high Mont Brouilly, an extinct volcano. The vineyards planted against it have their own *appellation*, that of the cru *Côte de Brouilly*. The wine has its own personality: an aroma of flowers and red fruits and berries plus quite a bit of alcohol. It is one of the strongest wines of Beaujolais. Parts of the districts of Cercié, Odenas, Quincié-en-Beaujolais and Saint-Lager belong to the cru. Other parts of the four villages are included in another cru, *Brouilly*. This encompasses the surroundings of Mont Brouilly and is about four times as large. Brouilly is also the largest of all the Beaujolais crus. Aside

Recommended Producers

Domaine Condemine Charming Brouilly.
Jean Lathuilière Often crowned.
Domaine Ruet Exquisite Brouilly.

Charentay

Château du Grand Vernay Côte de Brouilly and Beaujolais.
Domaine de Vuril Firm Brouilly.

Odenas

Château de la Chaize Vital Brouilly.
Bernard Champier Strikingly good Brouilly.
Guy Cotton Côte de Brouilly and Brouilly.
Domaine Crét des Garanches Brouilly.
Claudius Guérin Côte de Brouilly.
Château Thivin Exemplary wines.

from the four districts already mentioned, the territory encompasses land in Charentay and Saint-Etienne-la-Varenne. The wine has quite a few variants, but fruit and firmness are almost always present. Côte de Brouilly and Brouilly have a collective festival, which takes place on the first Saturday of September, on top of Mont Brouilly.

The southern slope of Mont Brouilly.

All the villages of Côte de Brouilly and Brouilly have their own charm. From the direction of Régnié, a visit could begin in *Quincié-en-Beaujolais* with its cream-coloured church, large co-operative and the imposing 15th-century castle of Varennes (along the road to Marchampt).

An inn in Saint-Lager.

Country hotel for those whose demands are simple. The rooms (about FF 180) are clean, but do not have a toilet. It is also a bar and simple restaurant. Near the church square.

RESTAURANTS

L'Auberge du Pont des Samsons
Quincié-en-Beaujolais
✆ 74.04.32.09
On the D 37, but looks nice. Menus start at about FF 70. The cuisine is regional with, for example, *coq au vin de Brouilly* and *demi coquelet aux écrevisses.*

Le Relais Beaujolais
Cercié
✆ 74.66.19.51
On the main street. Reasonably priced, rural dishes such as *jambonnette de canard au Brouilly* and *faux filet au Brouilly*. Nice assort-

QUINCIÉ-EN-BEAUJOLAIS
Cellier des Samsons Owned by 10 co-operatives.
Domaine Pavillon de Chavannes Côte de Brouilly.
SAINT-ETIENNE-LA-VARENNE
Domaine du Levant Reliable Brouilly.
Albert Sothier Supple, firm Brouilly.
Château des Tours Extensive estate.
SAINT-LAGER
Alain Bernillon Firm Côte de Brouilly.
l'Ecluse/Lucien et Robert Verger Côte de Brouilly.
Domaine du Griffon Very reliable.

ment of Brouillys. Menus start at about FF 155.

Auberge de Saint-Lager
Saint-Lager
✆ 74.66.82.30
When the weather is good you can eat outside on the rear terrace. Various menus under FF 100. The Menu Touristique usually offers good value for money (often with *coq au vin de Brouilly*).

Monique et Jean-Paul Crozier
Saint-Lager
✆ 74.66.82.79
Good place for a nutritious, tasty meal or a rich *salade Beaujolaise*. Five course menu at around FF 100. Unpretentious interior and a small terrace in front. It is also a bar.

Christian Mabeau
Odenas
✆ 74.03.41.79
The best restaurant of either cru. Talented cooks. The *à la carte* dishes are generally somewhat more progressive than those on the menus. The most inexpensive weekday menu is around FF 125. Terrace.

You come into *Cercié* by way of the D 37. The oldest building there is a 10th-century chapel. Go next to *Saint-Lager* where you will find various small castles and the *Cuvage des Brouilly* (the tasting room of both crus). *Charentay* has the ruins of the castle of Arigny and (along the road to Odenas) the 19th-century Tour de Belle-Mère. On the way to *Odenas* you look straight at Mont Brouilly. Further on, to the left, is the 17th-century Château de Pierreux. Château de la Chaize is actually much grander. It is situated in a large park on the south side of the village and is the creation of Mansart and Le Nôtre (of Versailles fame). The interior (Louis XIV) and the wine cellar are impressive. *Saint-Etienne-la-Varenne* is a picturesque village built on terraces.

Café in Quincié.

Vineyards near Odenas.

Southern Beaujolais

The southern part of Beaujolais comprises both flat and pronouncedly hilly areas. The wines here are Beaujolais Villages and Beaujolais (in red, white and rosé). It is worth the effort of exploring this varied territory with its beautiful and attractive villages, for example, via the following route. It begins with a short excursion to *Beaujeu*, which is situated to the west of the region, along the D 37. The centre consists of a long street, which runs past the church of Saint-Nicolas (Romanesque, 12th-century), a good place to park. Nearby you will find the tasting room of Beaujolais Villages: the Temple of Bacchus. Next to it is the city hall, which houses the *syndicat d'initiative* and the Musée des Arts et Traditions Populaires. Across from the church there is a half-timbered building which accommodates the Maison du Pays de Beaujeu et Haut-Beaujolais –

The interesting village of Vaux-en-Beaujolais.

Hotels

Château des Loges
Le Perréon
✆ 74.03.27.12
Small castle hotel (10 rooms, about FF 350) with adequate comfort and rather modern furnishings. It is also a restaurant. Le Perréon is situated not far from Vaux-en-Beaujolais.

Hostellerie Saint-Vincent
Salles-Arbuissonnas
✆ 74.67.55.50
This hotel, situated by an intersection, has a park, swimming pool and tennis court. The rooms are better than average (starting at about FF 300) and you can eat well here: *confit de canard maison, suprême de caille,* etc. Menus start at around FF 140.

Le Saint-Romain
Asne
✆ 74.68.05.89
The 24 rooms of this pleasant hotel (starting at approximately FF 200) have a rather classic interior, but are supplied with modern comfort. Peacefully situated a few kilometres from the exit off the autoroute. It is also a restaurant.

Recommended Producers

Beaujeu

Thomas la Chevalière Wine merchant. The best wine types, such as Domaine du Château de Saint-Jean (Beaujolais Villages) and Domaine de Creusenoire (white Beaujolais) bear an estate name.

Blace

Paul Gauthier The ordinary Beaujolais Villages and Beaujolais, as well as the primeur versions, have a lot of fruit and a pure, balanced taste.

Georges Texier & Fils Attractive Beaujolais Villages.

Restaurants

Anne de Beaujeu
Beaujeu
✆ 74.04.87.58
The cooking here is tasty, with a regional accent (*poulet de Bresse à la crème légère*). The most inexpensive menu – with a dish of the day – costs less than FF 115. There are also seven hotel rooms, with variable bathroom facilities. There is a car park in front of the hotel and a larger one 60 metres further up.

Auberge de Clochemerle
Vaux-en-Beaujolais
✆ 74.03.20.16
Rural inn with regional specialities *(terrines, coq au vin)*, fresh fish and a few surprising dishes (mainly à la carte). The owner is also a domestic caterer. Menus start at under FF 100.

Auberge de Liergues
Liergues
✆ 74.68.07.02
You eat here above a cafe on the church square. The portions are large, the prices good (menus begin under FF 100) and the style of cuisine is mainly regional.

an exhibition space with a store. From Beaujeu you come, by way of the D 37 (easterly) and the D 43 (southerly), to Odenas (see the previous chapter) and *Saint-Etienne-des-Ouillières* with its 19th-century Château de Lacarelle, the largest wine estate of Beaujolais. Now drive by way of *Le Perréon* – the co-operative has a good cellar for tasting wine in the Château des Loges (also a hotel-restaurant) – to *Vaux-en-Beaujolais.* This charming hill village was the backdrop for the novel *Clochemerle* by Gabriel Chevallier. Near the Romanesque church is the subject of Chevallier's book: a urinal, the most luxurious in Beaujolais. Near the Musée Viticole et Agricole (next to the church, in a sidestreet) another is situated. Black, metal signs point the way to stores and craftsmen in Vaux. From Vaux, take the marvellous, winding road to *Salles-Arbuissonas* (spectacular view). Park near the city hall and walk through a gateway to the church and the 10th-century monas-

In Beaujeu, after which Beaujolais is named.

Blaceret
La Folie Good reputation due to its fruity Brouilly.
Gobet Wine merchant with various qualities of Beaujolais. One of the best is that of the Domaine des Grandes Tours.

Le Breuil
Charmet Impeccable, fruity Beaujolais Cuvée la Centenaire. The white is also very successful.

Charnay
Domaine des Terres Dorées Beaujolais rich in fruit.

Chatillon-d'Azergues
Les Vins Mathelin Wine merchant. Delicious, supple, fruity wines.

tery, founded by the monks of Cluny. In the chapter house there are frescos to admire and, next to the church, a fine, peaceful cloister. To the east of Salles, *Blaceret* has a good regional restaurant. Leave this village and go on to *Blacé* with its 19th-century castle, then further south to *Cogny*, where the 12th-century church is built from an ochre-coloured stone that is characteristic of southern Beaujolais: *pierres dorées*, from which the route also derives its name. *Lierques* is the next stop. It has a good co-operative and an interesting church, with frescos and stone statuettes of craftsmen and a winegrower. By way of a route in the form of a loop (first north, then south) we now go on to *Buisante*. The hill there offers a fantastic panorama, a restaurant, a 19th-century chapel and an old cannon. Then on to *Pommiers*. In the 15th-century church curious, stone animal heads may be seen. After a small detour in a southwesterly direction, you reach *Anse*, which has Roman mosaics in the Château de Tours. Then drive by way of *Lachassagne* – for the view and the art gallery of La Cuvée – back onto the D 70 to *Charnay*. There are 'golden stones' galore here, as well as a 13th-century church (with a giant, multicoloured statue of Saint-Christophe) and a castle

The famous urinoir of Vaux.

Restaurant du Beaujolais
Blaceret
✆ 74.67.54.75
A restaurant overgrown with ivy, which has a terrace. Large menu with attractive dishes, including many regional ones. *A pot au feu* is usually on the menu one day in the week. Menus start at about FF 130.

Le Donjon
Oingt
✆ 74.71.20.24

LIERGUES
Cave Co-opérative Exquisite Beaujolais.
LE PERRÉON
Château des Loges The name of the better Beaujolais Villages from the local co-operative.
Domaine de la Madone Reliable Beaujolais Villages.
POMMIERS
Domaine Albert White and red Beaujolais.
SALLES-ARBUISSONAS
René et Christian Miolane Beaujolais Villages, usually of excellent quality.
SAINT-ETIENNE-DES-OUILLIERES
René Balandras Really delicious Beau-

Pleasant eating-house with a terrace (fine view). Rural dishes such as *confit de canard.* Menus start at approx. FF 100.

Le Savigny
Blacé
✆ 74.67.52.07
Stylish establishment where the cuisine is classic and delicious. Menus start at about FF 150. It is also a small hotel with nine nice rooms (starting at approx. FF 300).

La Terrasse des Beaujolais
Buisante
✆ 74.65.05.27
You have a magnificent view across southern Beaujolais. Simple, inexpensive dishes, strictly regional. Buisante is situated not far from Pommiers.

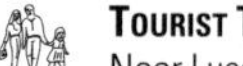

Tourist Tip
Near Lucenay, a village slightly south of Asne, is Le Golf du Beaujolais. The course consists of two circuits of 18 and 19 holes respectively and a club house in an 18th-century building. After the end of 1993 there will also be a hotel.

(also the city hall). A beautiful road runs to *Châtillon-d'Azarques.* Above this village looms a large castle. One of its chapels has wall paintings. Now go further northwest, along the D 485. *Le Breuil* is a fortified village with a castle. Turn right, a little further on, to *Le Bois d'Oingt*, the 'city of roses', and take the beautiful D 120 to

Vineyards in their autumn finery.

Middle-Age *Oingt.* This attractive little place (in part a national monument) has two castles. The central tower can be climbed and offers a marvellous view. A visit to the ancient hill village of *Ternand* makes an excellent finish. The archbishops of Lyon had their summer residences here. In the crypt of the 15th-century church, frescos from the Carolingian era can be admired.

jolais Villages.
Château de Lacarelle The ordinary Beaujolais Villages generally has a lively, fruity taste.
Domaine des Grandes Bruyères Nice Beaujolais Villages.
Vaux-en-Beaujolais
Château de Vaux Good Beaujolais.

Related to wine
- On the second Sunday in December the wines of the Hospices de Beaujeu itself are auctioned.
- The same Beaujeu also has a large, annual fair with a gastronomic element, held on the last Sunday of April.

INDEX

1. Producers, wine merchants etc.

Page numbers printed in *italics* indicate pages where the subject under consideration is dealt with more comprehensively. Abbreviations used:
Dom. (Domaine),
Ch. (Château).

2. Hotels